FRONT COVER: The Corney Fell Road (picture by Richard Harris)

OTHER BOOKS BY RICHARD HARRIS

BONGO NIGHTS

To celebrate the freedom he enjoyed on his retirement Richard Harris decided to spend a night in his ancient Bongo campervan every week for a year.

So for the next 52 weeks – all through the summer, autumn, winter and spring, and through sun, rain, gales, ice and snow – he set off once a week in his ancient Bongo van. Just because he could.

He went to places he'd never dreamed of going, did things he'd never dreamed of doing and met people he had never dreamed of meeting.

It was an extraordinary, exciting, dramatic and emotional year . . .

'Thoroughly enjoyed every minute of reading this. This is a good read regardless of whether you own a campervan or not'

'What a great read! Some truly laugh out loud moments'

BUS PASS TO ETERNITY

Starting in the bedroom in which he was born, and helped by the host of memorable characters he meets along the way, Richard Harris recreates an emotional journey through the places that were important to him as he grew up and began to carve out a career as a journalist.

Beginning in South Devon, and ending in the woodland cemetery near Carlisle in which he already has a plot booked, the journey takes in all the places that have mattered most to him.

And he does it all for nothing – travelling every one of the 865 miles for free, using only his old folk's bus pass

'He has such a talent for making the mundane seem to interesting'

'What a lovely book. Nostalgic, funny . . . and beautiful writing'

Find them on www.richardharrisnews.co.uk

BONGO NIGHTS

2

A-Z of the Lake District

A celebration of (responsible) wildcamping
in the best bit of Britain

www.richardharrisnews.co.uk

Richard Harris
CA8 9JY
UK

ISBN: 978-1-71640710-9

'People don't take trips,
trips take people'

John Steinbeck

PREFACE

BEFORE you join me on my wanderings around this most beautiful part of Britain I need to tell you a little about what you have let yourself in for.

Not least because much of it is, technically, against the law.

This book is about some of the unforgettable nights I have spent in my ancient campervan in the Lake District – beautiful, wonderful, awe-inspiring places every one, and places that deserve to be experienced by anyone who loves the sort of untamed beauty and remoteness that this special corner of Britain offers . . . but places in which, technically again, I had no right to be.

The fact is that in most places in England and Wales (though not in Scotland, where attitudes are perhaps more enlightened) it is not strictly legal just to park a van in a layby and spend the night in it.

Because every square inch of the country is owned by *somebody*, permission has to be sought before we can lawfully park a van or pitch a tent on their land and go to sleep there.

I have never quite understood the reasoning that allows me to park in some wild and out-of-the-way place in the hours of daylight but bans me from doing exactly the same thing in exactly the same place once the sun has gone down.

I have never quite understood the distinction . . . but I accept that there is one.

One is called 'parking' (and is positively encouraged by the tourism industry, especially if I happen to buy an ice cream from the corner shop or a pint from the village pub) and the other has come to be called 'wildcamping' (which, strictly, is against the law no matter how many ice creams or pints of beer I might buy to help the local economy while I'm doing it).

You will notice that I use words like 'technically' and 'strictly'. That is because until now it has never mattered very much what the law says. There has long been a healthy tradition of both sides turning a blind eye to the rules – a good old British compromise that says they won't bother us if we don't bother them.

Even in the Lake District, camping in laybys and on grass verges has been tolerated despite the fact that for more than 20 years a National Park Authority bye-law has banned the overnight parking of campervans in anywhere other than an official campsite.

It is – or has been for many years – something that has been looked upon as part of the tourism landscape, by landowners as much as by visitors.

It is true that some wildcamping campervanners have let the side down, causing noise and nuisance and leaving rubbish and ruining the very thing that, presumably, they have come to see.

They don't seem to realise that wildcamping, whether in a campervan or a tent, is a privilege, not a right, and if we can't do it without upsetting other people we shouldn't do it at all.

But they are a very small minority and, believe me, I am not one of them.

I like to think I have standards; I have rules, and so, I believe, do most other wildcampers.

When I stay somewhere in my campervan I don't leave a trace – not even a tyre mark in the mud, if I can help it.

I never park within sight of a house, or another campervan, and if I find a sign telling me that overnight parking is banned I simply move on to some place where it isn't.

I make no noise, I light no fires and I create no disturbance in any way.

And – because I always take a binbag with me, to collect any litter that other people have left there – I always leave a place tidier than I found it.

If that makes me some sort of goody-two-shoes among wildcampers, so be it.

I have loved the freedom and the solitude, the tranquillity and the beauty and it is no exaggeration to say that some of the nights I have spent wildcamping in my campervan have been among the best nights of my life.

But in late July 2020 everything changed . . . and, though it pains me to say it, it did so for the best of reasons.

When travel restrictions were lifted after the great pandemic lockdown, the Lake District saw an influx of tourists like it had never seen before.

Thousands upon thousands of them headed to this most beautiful of Britain's beautiful places and many – too many – came in campervans and motorhomes.

And, naturally, because people knew that wildcamping had long been tolerated here, many of them chose to stay not in formal campsites (most of which were full anyway) but on any suitable bit of land they could find.

The result was chaos.

On one night alone 118 vans homed in on Buttermere, an area singularly unequipped to deal with such an onslaught.

The authorities, not surprisingly, decided they had to do something.

So they invoked the by-law that they had never previously much bothered with, and banned the overnight occupation of any vehicle in anywhere where camping was not officially allowed.

And, just to emphasise that they were serious, they got the police to tour the area, telling people to move on if they found them settling down for the night in their campervans and threatening them with hefty fines if they were caught trying it again.

As someone who for a long time has loved wildcamping – waking up in some remote place with the sun shining through the windows, with no other human being for miles around and the dawn chorus the only sound – that was a huge disappointment to me.

But as someone who loves the Lake District, who lives just up the road from it and so is lucky enough to be able to enjoy it all year round, I could not argue with it.

The beauty and magic of the Lakes is too precious to risk it being spoiled, even by people like me.

There's no escaping the fact that the ban on wildcamping did have an effect on this book though.

When I started writing it, it had three aims:

1: To give me some fun

2: To describe the pleasure of being able to park a campervan freely in some of this country's most wonderful places, and

3: To show people (including those who prefer to spend their nights in formal campsites, hotels and B&Bs) that with a good map and a bit of imagination it is still possible for them to spend their days in fantastic Lake District locations far away from the tourist hordes.

And somewhere along the way a fourth aim raised its head:

To show the authorities that wildcamping in campervans can be done responsibly . . . and that, once the urgency of post Covid19 tourism has passed, it will be possible to turn that blind eye towards it once again.

RICHARD HARRIS
Cumbria
November 2020

INTRODUCTION

IT IS DIFFICULT to overstate the impact my Bongo has had on my life. Who would have thought that a humble and ancient campervan could contribute so much?

The Bongo – that's not the name I chose to call mine, but the one Mazda, the makers, gave the model when it first rolled off their production line in May 1995 – is a magical little vehicle, often described as the most versatile on the road.

Bongos are people carriers – originally designed as mobile offices-cum-hotel-rooms for commercial travellers in Japan – big enough to provide reasonably spacious accommodation for two people but, unlike their huge motorhome cousins, small enough to go anywhere a typical family car can go, and they have become something of a cult in Britain, among people with (I like to think) a bit of a hippyish taste for doing things just a little bit differently.

At 25 years old mine is one of the oldest you will see, but I like to think it is one of the best equipped. It has been converted into a campervan (complete with cooker, fridge, sink, cupboards and pull-out bed) and it has brought me untold pleasure and adventure since I bought it from a dealer in Scotland nearly ten years ago.

In my first 'Bongo Nights' book I told how I had the crazy idea of camping in the Bongo one night a week for 52 consecutive weeks.

That seemed a great idea in the warm sunshine of summer when I started, but perhaps less so in the driving rain of autumn and the ice and snow of winter, but I stuck to my task and 12 months later was able to celebrate the completion of my mission with a party on one of the steamers that ply their trade on Ullswater, my favourite lake.

In that year I inadvertently slept in two places associated with murder, spent a night in a Buddhist temple after passing an hour in the company of a dead nun, fled in embarrassment when my chosen Bongo spot was taken over by members of the local dogging community, and spent 14 hours on an Irish headland where there was nothing between me and the coast of Nova Scotia except 3,000 miles of sea. . . .

There really is nothing better than waking up in the Bongo, all alone in some remote but beautiful spot, with just the calling of the birds and the baa-ing of a distant sheep for company.

Fifty-two weeks, 52 nights and 52 very special places.

It was one of the most extraordinary years of my life . . . and I couldn't wait to do it all (or something very similar) again.

But this time, I decided, I would be rather more focused.

Instead of travelling to an exciting myriad of places in England, Scotland, Wales and Ireland – most of them for no better reason than I wanted to – this time I would confine myself to just one area.

The place just down the road, the place I know best. The Lake District.

I would find 26 places – some well-known, most not. Starting with somewhere beginning with A, then B, then C . . . and ending with Z – and I would spend one night in each of them.

Twenty-six places, 26 one-night holidays, 26 adventures . . .

It would be my Bongo Nights A-Z Guide to the Lake District.

How I enjoyed it!

I hope you do too . . .

1

Ambleside

The Land Rover was upside down, balanced on its roof on the far side of a rubble-strewn gap in the dry stone wall.

It was impossible to tell whether there was anyone still inside, alive or dead. The quick glance I was able to give it as I drove up the hill was enough only to tell me that inside it was a jumble of what looked like sleeping bags and blankets.

A steady stream of traffic was coming down the hill, in the same direction that the Land Rover had obviously come, but apart from one car which slowed slightly as it passed, none of the drivers appeared to react in any way.

I was past it in a flash, on my way up the Kirkstone Pass, heading for the little town of Ambleside, where I planned to spend the first of my A-Z nights in my Bongo and initially I dismissed the crashed Land Rover as just another vehicle belonging to someone whose driving skills were not up to the challenges presented by the Lake District's mountain roads.

But as I drove on, towards the summit of the hill, where tourists park in the big lay-by opposite the Kirkstone Pass Inn to take selfies of themselves against a dramatic background of Red Screes or Caudale Moor. I began to wonder.

I was assuming that the Land Rover had been there for some time and that the occupants were long gone, safe, apart from the odd bruise or fracture maybe, and probably regaling their friends at that very moment with tales of their miraculous escape from a terrifying crash,

But then I thought . . . I had seen no sign of any comforting blue and white 'Police Aware' tape as I had driven past.

So what if the crash had only just happened?

What if even now there was still someone in that Land Rover – someone perhaps just clinging on to life, slumped over the shattered steering wheel, and praying that someone would bring help soon?

What if it was a whole family – Mum and Dad dead or unconscious in the front, and two terrified children in the back, protected by the softness of the sleeping bags as the vehicle had somersaulted through the wall?

I knew I could not go on and enjoy my night in Ambleside without making sure there was not still someone trapped in the wreckage.

So I found a handy place to turn around and headed back down the hill.

I pulled up beside the smashed wall, just a few yards from the Land Rover, turned on my hazard warning lights and climbed out.

The Land Rover had clearly hit the wall with some force, though why it should have done so on a relatively straight stretch of road was something of a mystery.

I peered at the vehicle on the other side and saw that, other than being upside down, there was little wrong with it.

It was impossible to tell how many people had been – or still were – in it, because the mess of what I now saw were blankets, pillows and sleeping bags seemed to fill it entirely.

I was resigned to going closer, to open a door and find . . . who knew what?

But then I noticed a torn piece of paper, somehow fixed to the inside of the rear passenger window, with a note written in pencil: 'POLICE AWARE'.

I returned to the Bongo, my emotions jumbled – relieved that nobody appeared to have been hurt but annoyed that I had felt myself compelled to make an unnecessary journey to discover that that was so.

My plan – now slightly delayed – was straightforward. I would leave the Bongo somewhere in Ambleside (I had timed my arrival for after 5pm so that I would be able to park on-street for as long as I liked), go for a walk, find a pub for my supper and, just as it was getting dark, drive a mile or so up the hill known as The Struggle, to a handy parking place which I knew would, when the sun came up next morning, provide me with splendid views over Windermere.

Ambleside is a great place for a man with a Bongo – several nice pubs, plenty of good walks, lots to do even if it's raining and, best of all, a wide choice of verges, lay-bys and rough areas in which to park a van overnight.

I did almost a full lap of the town before finding a parking space outside the Co-op in Compston Road, just a short walk from Zeffirellis, one of Ambleside's two cinemas.

It would be extraordinary enough for a town the size of Ambleside (it has a population of only 3,000, though of course that can multiply tenfold at the height of the tourist season) to have even one cinema, but Ambleside has two – and two that provide a total of five screens at that.

Zeffirellis (it has no apostrophe, by order of the owners) was founded by former rock-band drummer Derek Hook nearly 40 years ago in what had previously been a 'flea-pit' cinema.

Since then it has expanded into an old school just down the road, and been joined by its sister Fellinis, a three-minute walk away, which was set up in 2010 in what had been the Conservative Club.

Both are attached to very successful restaurants and have become welcome institutions in a town renowned more for its outdoor than its artistic culture.

It had not been in my mind to visit either establishment that night, but when I found myself parking almost right outside Zeffirellis it was enough to make me rejig my plans for the evening.

Since the films all started at about 8pm I decided still to go for a walk, but to be back in town for 7.45, to give me a quarter of an hour to decide which one to watch.

That would allow me an hour for my supper in one of the many pubs . . . as long as I took no more than 70 minutes walking, 35 minutes there and 35 minutes back.

On the street corner right in front of me a signpost pointed me to Rothay Park and Loughrigg, so I grabbed my cagoule and set off, knowing that in precisely 35 minutes I would simply turn around and come back again.

The route took me on a pleasant stroll down a quiet street, across a park, over a wonderful ancient bridge, a short distance up a road . . . and then up a narrow lane that seemed to ascend almost vertically up the side of a mountain.

I enjoy walking enormously, but I am not one of nature's fellwalkers – largely on account of the fact that I don't see much point in toiling uphill for hours just to have a quick look at the view (if you're lucky and it's not obliterated by drizzle, that is) and walk back down again.

So my slog up that hill through the woods on the way towards Loughrigg was, while no doubt being a very good workout, not especially enjoyable.

Eventually the path brought me out onto the open fell, levelled off and I was at last able to catch my breath.

I looked at my watch.

It had taken me 34 minutes. I had just one minute to enjoy walking on the flat before turning round and walking back down the hill again.

I had not seen any living thing on my way up the hill, but almost as soon as I turned back I found myself facing three deer, eyeing me with suspicion from the side of the path.

I stopped and they stopped, and after a minute or so they gave a little flick of their heads and wandered off slowly into the trees.

And then suddenly I was walking against the tide.

It was the time of day when the more energetic people of Ambleside take their dogs for a walk.

The first was a middle-aged lady with a spaniel trotting cheerfully beside her on a lead.

The second was slightly younger, with a collie bounding all over the road as it came around a bend about 20 yards ahead of me.

She said something quietly and the dog stopped, crossed the road back to her and, without any need for a lead or further instruction, quietly took its position and followed at her heel.

Now, I have no great love of dogs. In fact with one or two notable exceptions I can't stand them.

And their owners – especially those who simper 'He's only being friendly' when their objectionable mutt jumps up and tries to lick my face or have sex with my leg – I like even less.

But this one was clearly different.

'Thank you very much,' I said. 'It's so good to see such a well behaved dog.'

She smiled and said 'He knows he's not allowed to be anything else' in a voice so soft and sultry I almost crossed the road and followed at her heel myself.

Four teenagers, aged about 14 and loaded with supermarket shopping as if they were planning to cook their supper in a tent they had left up on the fell, were next, strung out in a line as they came puffing up the hill.

'Hello,' I said to each of them.

'Hi,' said the two girls.

'Hi,' said the first boy, his cheeks pink with exertion.

'Good afternoon,' said the second, in a gravelly baritone surely far too deep to have come from someone so young.

I fear I visibly jumped and turned round in surprise as he passed, and found him turning round too to give me the smile of a boy who is well used to strangers doing a double take on hearing him speak.

The walk back to Ambleside was more interesting – and a good deal easier – than the walk away from it had been and I was back at the Bongo well inside my 35 minute time limit.

After changing out of my walking boots and waterproof trousers (a Bongo with its heavily tinted windows makes an excellent changing room) I searched my mobile phone for some advice on where to eat.

'Best pub in Ambleside?' I typed.

'The Unicorn,' it replied.

The Unicorn, just off the town centre in North Road, is Ambleside's oldest pub and, from my experience of a previous visit, one of its friendliest.

I bought myself a pint of Unicorn (it seemed neatly appropriate to choose a beer which, coincidentally, shared the name of the pub), settled down at one of the few vacant tables while I waited for my scampi and chips and soon found myself in conversation with a nearby couple whose male half was awaiting a mixed grill that he knew from the night before would be 'bloody enormous'.

'Best food in the Lake District,' he told me with, I thought, a touch of exaggeration.

He told me that he came from Yorkshire and that they had been coming to the same B&B in Ambleside for more than ten years although what they really wanted now was a campervan.

I told him of my Bongo and the night I was planning to spend in it no more than a mile from where we were speaking and I detected a look of envy in his eyes.

He told me that as he had been 'in transport' all his life (he was a lorry driver) he would feel more at home in a campervan than he ever did in a guesthouse, and he would particularly enjoy setting off to find somewhere wild to park for the night after having a few pints in a pub.

This brought us on to a subject I have always been wary about while Bongoing: When, legally, can a man be said to be 'in charge' of a vehicle? Or, to put it another way, can you be charged with drink driving even if your only intention is to go to sleep?

The law says that it's an offence to 'drive, attempt to drive, or be in charge of a motor vehicle on a road or public place if the level of alcohol in your breath, blood or urine exceeds the prescribed limit' – and, for anyone sleeping overnight in a campervan, the important words there are 'in charge of'.

My own feeling is that a driver sleeping the night in a campervan is still in charge of it, and is therefore subject to drink-driving rules.

All it needs is some jobsworth policeman (and yes, there are such things) to come beating on your door in the middle of the night and, if you've previously sunk a few pints in the pub, you could be in trouble.

I have some experience in this regard.

In my time as a court reporter one of my most unusual cases was of a man found guilty of driving a car while disqualified . . . even though it did not have an engine.

One of his mechanic friends had taken the engine out while renovating the car and the two of them were pushing the shell of the vehicle down the road to somewhere where more work could be done on it.

When they reached the brow of a small hill the car started running away, so our man jumped into the driver's seat and pulled on the handbrake to stop it.

A passing policeman, knowing the man had previously been banned from driving, booked him for driving while disqualified and, though he pleaded not guilty on the grounds that a car without an engine was surely not a motor vehicle, he was convicted.

If that can happen, I reckon, a sleeping man could surely also be found to be 'in charge' of a campervan and duly convicted of drink-driving.

'That's why I'm always careful not to drink too much when I'm out in my Bongo,' I told the lorry driver in the Unicorn. 'It's just not worth taking the risk.'

'Nah,' he said. 'It's just an old wives' tale. You'd be fine.'

'Like I said, it's not worth taking the risk,' I said as he turned his attention to the huge plateful of pork chop, sausage, black pudding, bacon, baked beans, onion rings, grilled tomatoes and chips that had just arrived on his table.

A pleasant walk through Ambleside took me back to Zeffirellis and – on discovering that I did not fancy any of the films on offer there that night – on to Fellinis, where I bought a ticket for what looked like being the least bad film (Wild River, a very violent murder mystery set in the snowy wastes of Wyoming) on offer in the town that night.

Afterwards I drove up to my chosen parking place – a large level area beside the road that leads up to the Kirkstone Pass – hoping all the way that no other campervan had got there first.

I was in luck. Nobody was there. When I got out of the van I looked up and saw for the first time that the sky was clearer than it had been for months. There were no clouds. And no electric lights to intrude on the darkness. It was just me and a million stars.

I woke early next morning with the sun spearing through a gap in the curtains, and got up immediately, eager to see the view down over Windermere.

The sky above my hilltop eyrie was clear blue, the wind gently warm . . . and below me I couldn't see a thing. The valley had been blocked out by a thick morning mist, with only the spire of Ambleside church poking up into the sunshine, as if beckoning me down to the lake.

I needed no further invitation.

Spending a day at the lake was what I had in mind anyway.

I drove back down to Ambleside, parked the Bongo in an unrestricted parking place that I had found on my walk the previous evening, and walked a mile to the pier at Waterhead, where the lake cruises arrive and depart.

I was going to do something I had been meaning to do for almost all the 28 years I had lived in Cumbria.

'Good choice,' said the man at the Windermere Lake Cruises ticket office when I asked for a Walker's Ticket. 'It's a great day for it.'

A small launch would take me on the 15 minute trip to the far side of the lake, and from there I would walk for four miles along the Windermere shore to catch two more boats to bring me back to where I had started.

I had not intended to bother visiting Wray Castle, but since the boat took me virtually to its front door I couldn't bring myself to ignore it.

Wray Castle is a mock gothic mansion built in the 1840s by a wealthy Liverpool surgeon as his retirement home and is not like any other National Trust property I have known.

And though I hate to argue with William Wordsworth (he said it 'added a dignified feature to the interesting scenery in the midst of which it stands') I find myself agreeing with all the people who, since the day it was built, have described it as a bit of a blot on the landscape.

And I couldn't disagree either with the wife of the wealthy surgeon who, on seeing what her husband had had built with her inheritance from a gin fortune, apparently refused to live in it.

Unusual, yes. Surprising, yes. Interesting, maybe. But beautiful?

It is only a shell, for a start, with a maze of rooms arranged around a huge central tower which must have made the place impossible to heat.

There is no furniture, apart from a pingpong table and a billiard table (with hideously torn baize) which visitors are invited to play on

From 1958 to 1998 it was a training college for Merchant Navy officers, so I might once have found myself living there had I not as a 15-year-old changed my mind and opted against the seafaring career that had been my ambition since early childhood.

I can't say I'm too disappointed at having missed the chance.

I found little to interest me in Wray Castle and did not waste much time before leaving it.

Perhaps the reason I did not take to Wray was that it was a lovely day and I was more in the mood for walking beside the lake than exploring a cold and dingy not-really-a-castle.

And I was right. The walk along the west shore of Windermere is a great way of getting some gentle exercise in one of the most beautiful parts of the country.

The undulating path is easy and well maintained – the sort that gets you whistling a happy ditty to yourself as you stride along – and there are plenty of rocks and benches to sit on with a flask of tea to soak in the views.

I was approaching one of them when I saw an elderly couple ahead of me, doing something – precisely what was unclear at that distance – to a small black dog.

As I got closer I saw that she was holding it firmly by its shoulders, while he was busy at the other end, holding its tail with one hand and using a tissue to wipe its arse with the other.

'Good morning,' I said in a voice which probably had something of a questioning tone to it.

But they were too busy to reply.

Windermere is a lake I seldom go to, mainly because it boasts two of the Lake District's honeypots – Ambleside and Bowness – which are packed with tourists almost all through the year.

Much better, in my book, is Ullswater, which is even more beautiful, does not attract anything like the crowds . . . and, happily, is the closest of all the lakes to my home.

Ullswater is one of those rare places where it is possible still to find almost total silence.

Windermere, I discovered, is not.

As I strolled along its western shore I was conscious of the constant noise.

The busy main road on the far side did not help, of course, but the racket of shouting voices from passing boats and – worse – those boats' engines provided a constant noisy background to it.

I was beginning to wonder if it was just my inbuilt bolshiness – 'This isn't Ullswater so I'm going to find as many things I don't like as I can' – when I fell into conversation with a fellow walker waiting at Ferry House for the small boat to take us across the lake to Bowness-on-Windermere.

'Surprising how noisy it is, isn't it?' he said as a small motor boat chugged past.

This was Geoff from Liverpool, who was staying in Ambleside with his wife on, he told me, one of the rare holidays that did not involve his 30ft ocean going yacht.

'The only place I've found that you can find proper silence is off the west coast of Scotland,' he said. 'Everywhere else – even when you're at sea – you can hear the engine of some boat or ship throbbing away in the distance.'

He told me how he loved to take his boat through the Western Isles and watch the seals and otters playing on the rocks as he lay at anchor off some bay.

'You wouldn't swap your boat with any of those then?' I asked, nodding towards the fleet of yachts bobbing in front of us on the swell.

I took his dismissive 'Huh!' as a sign that he would not.

He confirmed it a few minutes later as our little ferry took us on a zig-zag course through the moored yachts on its way to Bowness.

'I reckon most of these are for show,' he said. 'I have a friend who hired a yacht here. He came home early because after four days he was bored. He'd been everywhere he could go and there was nowhere left. It's not exactly the open sea, is it?'

Bowness was exactly as I knew it would be: Buzzing with hordes of people having the time of their lives. But not quite my cup of tea.

There is nothing wrong with Bowness – apart from the number of people who go there – and it does me good to see it every now and then just to remind myself that it is only because some people enjoy such crowded places that people like me can be left free to enjoy the quiet spots where we have only the sound of the breeze and the birds for company.

I did not feel obliged to join in the fun, so as the ferry made its way towards the bustling pier I was relieved to see the unmistakable outline of MV Teal, the best of Windermere Lakes Cruises' boats, waiting there for me.

It meant I would have to spend no more than 15 minutes in Bowness, which was plenty.

And I spent five of them queuing for an ice cream.

I was still eating it when I joined the line of passengers, to be welcomed aboard the Teal by a smiling shirt-sleeved deckhand.

The Teal is a splendid boat, gleaming white with three decks and a tall wooden wheelhouse, giving it something of the appearance of a Mississippi riverboat.

It was built in Barrow-in-Furness in 1936, then taken apart and transported by rail the 30 miles to Bowness to be put back together there on the Lakeside.

I found myself a seat at the bow, alongside a couple from Birmingham who were busy tucking into a picnic that they had unloaded from a rucsac shaped like a badger.

'You on holiday?' the husband asked.

'Sort of,' I replied. 'But I live here in Cumbria so you could say that every day is a holiday.'

'Lucky bugger,' he said. 'So what are you doing here on this boat if you're local?'

'Going home,' I told him with a grin. 'I'll be home in less than two hours.'

And so I was.

The Teal soon deposited me at Ambleside, from where a short walk took me back to the Bongo. Then a drive through some of England's finest scenery took me home.

To a place where there was not a tourist to be seen.

2

Buttermere

It did not augur well for my next Bongo Night – in Buttermere – when I found the road leading there was closed.

Work being done to repair the damage caused by Storm Desmond, nearly two years before, had made the road from Keswick over the Newlands pass to Buttermere – one of the finest drives in the Lake District – impassable.

The diversion took me slightly further west, over the Whinlatter pass and along the shore of Crummock Water, instead, which was nearly as good a drive, and one that would have left any stranger awestruck and reaching for his camera at every turn, but it was simply not the one I had been intending and so for me, on that day, it was mildly disappointing.

Still, Buttermere is always a good place to come to, from whichever direction, and I arrived in happy enough mood despite the persistent drizzle that hid all the best views behind a grey mist.

There are car parks in Buttermere – one owned by the National Trust, just out of the village, and another by the Lake District National Park Authority, which is much nearer the lake and about as close as you can get to it without actually getting your feet wet – but many people, me included, seem to aim for a patch of rough ground just north of the church, along the road I would have come down had it not been closed.

I found a spot among a cluster of cars, none of which, I noticed, had a local number plate.

It seemed I would be spending my day with people from Manchester, Leeds, Gloucester, Derby and Stratford-upon-Avon (I particularly warmed to them, whoever they were, because anyone who turned their back on Shakespeare to enjoy a few days in the magic of the Lake District was all right by me).

I sat for a few minutes, debating with myself the wisdom of going for a walk in the rain compared with hunkering down in the Bongo dozing in the comfort of the driver's seat until the worst of it passed . . .

And strangely, the walk in the rain won.

'I am here to enjoy myself,' I reminded myself as I reached for my cagoule. 'So enjoy myself I will.'

And so I did until I stepped out onto the tarmac and my face experienced the afternoon's full wetness being blown into my face.

I looked around for somewhere to shelter and made an unseemly dash for the little church just down the hill.

St James' Church, Buttermere, is glorious even in the rain – a 19th century gem of a place of which William Wordsworth said: 'A man must be very unsensible who would not be touched at the sight' of it.

The dozen or so stone steps that took me up from the road onto the rocky plateau on which the church is built had become a waterfall beneath my feet and by the time I reached the porch beneath the little bell tower I was drenched.

I stood dripping inside and, in virtual darkness, gave a gentle push to the door in front of me.

Nothing happened, so I gave a more generous shove, then a full shoulder charge . . . and the door reluctantly creaked open to display a gorgeous little white chapel, whose simple beauty was accentuated by the heavy dark beams that stretched overhead like the skeleton of a boat.

In the window alcove to my left was a carved slate memorial to Alfred Wainwright, the renowned fellwalker who did more than anyone to make trekking over the Cumbrian mountains something that people in their thousands now want to do:

'Pause and remember Alfred Wainwright. Fellwalker, guidebook author and illustrator, who loved this valley. Lift your eyes to Haystacks, his favourite place.'

I did as I was told, looked out of the window, lifted my eyes as instructed and could see nothing but drizzle.

I spent many minutes in the church, sitting in the rearmost pew, simply enjoying the peace of the place, and for a while it didn't matter to me what the weather was doing outside.

I was dragged from my reverie by the sound of someone coming into the porch, followed by a haphazard scratching at the door.

Clearly the church's next visitors were having even more trouble opening the heavy door in the dark than I had had.

The scratching morphed into a rather more formal knocking.

Rat-tat-tat.

I got up and pulled, to give the door a helping hand, and peered around it into the blackness of the porch as it slowly opened.

'Do come in,' I said, in a voice more gravelly than I intended . . . and the small boy on the other side noticeably jumped and looked terrified as he saw me looming out of the darkness towards him, silhouetted against the light behind me.

'It's OK, I'm just going,' I told him and he stared at me, eyes wide and mouth open as if he had been confronted by God himself.

I had spent considerably longer than necessary in the church and had run out of reasons to stay.

So as the small boy came inside I took his place in the porch, zipped up my cagoule, pulled my hat tighter to my head and stepped outside into the wretchedness that awaited me there.

The weather was truly dreadful – the wind blowing the drizzle horizontally into my face, stinging the small areas of flesh protected by neither beard nor cagoule hood.

And – defying all those who would expect me, in such circumstances, to dive back into the Bongo for an afternoon with a good book – I set off towards Scale Force.

Scale Force, I knew, was one of the top sights to see in that area – the highest waterfall in the Lake District, where the water of Scale Beck tumbles all of 170ft vertically down a cliff in a deep tree-lined gorge.

My guidebook had told me it was a 'spectacular sight even after dry periods', and this was anything but a dry period, but even so those of my friends who know much more about the Lake District landscape than I do had warned me to expect to be disappointed.

William Wordsworth described it as 'a fine chasm, with a lofty, though but slender, fall of water' but he made no mention of its being hidden so deep among the trees that it was virtually invisible to anyone not actually standing in it.

The path that I took skirted a car park before crossing a field and cutting between two lakes – Buttermere and Crummock Water – and I remembered that on the better days on which I had walked along here before I had marvelled at the wonderful views in every direction.

Today though I just trudged onwards, following the path that went parallel to the grey outline of Crummock Water on my right, determinedly dodging the puddles that had turned the muddy path into a watery maze and lifting my eyes only long enough to nod sympathetically to a young couple – dripping and miserable-looking – I met along the way.

After a while the path swung around to the left, cutting half-heartedly through a forest of waist-high bracken before rising up towards an indistinct smudge among the trees that I took to be the waterfall.

Fifty yards or so ahead of me a man in a pale yellow cagoule was making heavy weather of a smaller path that seemed to be taking him into even denser undergrowth in completely the wrong direction.

I went carefully, picking my way along the path, making sure that one foot was firmly planted on solid ground before lifting the other in front of me.

On a previous Bongo Night I had broken my leg after slipping on a patch of wet grass, and I had no wish to repeat that experience – especially since here I was so far from both help and, I was guessing, the mobile phone signal that might have helped me call for it.

Eventually I came to a bridge, and then a zigzag path that appeared to be leading towards where I guessed the base of the waterfall must be and beneath me I spotted the man in the yellow cagoule diving once more into the bracken that almost enveloped him, making a new path for himself by vigorously swishing his walking pole in front of him.

I found my way to the waterfall, and stood there on a rock muttering a few words of agreement to the friends who had warned me that while Scale Force was the Lake District's biggest it was far from the best.

There seemed to be more water running down my neck than there was falling down the cliff in front of me and I stayed only long enough to curse the sheer pointlessness of it all.

I had taken only a few paces back down the hill when I heard the sound of something lumbering through the bracken.

It was the man in the yellow cagoule, emerging from the undergrowth on nothing that could be mistaken for a path, and from a direction he had no reason to be emerging from.

We passed within a few feet of each other – me on my path and he in his undergrowth – and I grunted 'Hello' while trying to make eye contact, but he walked straight on, as if in his determination to go where no man had gone before he had not seen me.

Reaching the Bongo, with the rain pelting on the roof, and the wind beginning to howl outside, I took off my dripping clothes, pulled on a thick sweater and a pair of dry trousers, propped myself against the bench seat in the back and closed my eyes.

I realised that the place in which I was parked was a reasonably satisfactory one for a night's stay – it was not quite level, but level enough, and quiet, and would be quieter still once the few remaining walkers had returned to their cars and gone home – but I had other ideas.

The Fish Inn was at the bottom of the hill, a very short distance away, and I knew that a pint and a hot bar meal were all I needed to restore my spirits.

I drove down (I had had enough of walking in the rain), parked the Bongo in a corner of the car park and went inside. The Fish is not a bad pub – it has the air of a well equipped village hall, but is comfortable and welcoming nonetheless – and I sat on the stool at the bar from which I judged I would best be able to develop a relationship with the landlord.

We chatted about the weather, waterproofs, beer and tourists . . . and, when I at last thought I had softened him up with my friendly repartee, eventually came to the point.

'How would you feel about me spending the night in my campervan in the corner of your car park?' I asked.

And I pointed out that I would then be able to have more than the single pint I had already had.

He shook his head.

'No, we don't allow that,' he said. 'It might disturb the guests in the bedrooms there.'

A fair enough reason, I told him.

'OK, thanks anyway. But it's always worth asking.'

He agreed that it was, but then added: 'Anyway, you'd find it a bit exposed down there.'

And, after a moment's thought: 'And anyway it's one of the conditions of our planning permission that we don't do that. We could get into a lot of trouble.'

Now, call me a cynic, but while I was happy to accept one reason, since being welcomed into a pub's car park is a luxury, not an entitlement, I got the feeling that by giving me three he was now over-egging it.

'OK,' I said. 'That's fine. I'll go back to my original plan.'

And I left before he had time to come up with another excuse.

That night I slept soundly in the Bongo parked in a small layby a little further up the hill, past the church and its not-quite-level parking place.

When I woke up next morning it was still raining.

Yet I fancied another walk.

This time I chose somewhere a bit flatter – one of the old coffin roads that abound in this area.

Coffin roads are usually nothing more than rough tracks, the route that people took to carry their dead from the remote villages in which they died to the churchyards in which they were to be buried. The one I chose was beside Loweswater – the next lake further down the valley from Buttermere and Crummock Water – which leads from Buttermere to Lamplugh church, and onwards to St Bees Priory.

The path struck up from a small car park, past a clump of trees, through a maze of dry stone walls and into a farmyard guarded, it seemed, by a pack of fierce dogs, which barked, growled and rattled their chains at me from all directions.

'Shut up you daft buggers,' said a man who ambled out through the decaying door of one of the barns.

Unlike his animals, the man was friendly.

He apologised for the dogs, and wondered aloud why they still worked themselves up into a state of such excitement whenever a stranger approached, since that was something that happened many times a day every day of the year including Christmas.

'It's a popular walk,' he said when I raised an eyebrow.

He told me his farm was owned by the National Trust, though his family had been tenants there for several generations.

'Are they good landlords?' I asked, not quite as innocently as I tried to sound.

I knew that the National Trust had recently got themselves into an almighty tangle by paying way over the asking price for a farm in another part of the Lake District, thereby falling out with the local community, many of whom had hoped to buy it themselves but found themselves unable to compete with the Trust's apparently bottomless pockets.

'They used to be,' he told me.

I said nothing, hoping that he would be encouraged to fill the silence with an explanation.

'Trouble is they've all been to college these days and they think they know everything.

'In my father's day, and my grandfather's, they trusted us to do things right because they knew we knew what we were doing.

'These days experience counts for nothing, so they who've been to college think they know better than we who've grown up on this land and have been doing the job – and doing it well – all our lives.'

I gave him a look that I was confident was sympathetic.

'It's difficult,' he said. 'Aye, difficult.'

He opened a gate for me and sent me on my way, wishing me a happy day despite the rain.

3
The Corney Fell Road

There is – or, rather, was – somewhere in the Lake District that I had heard mentioned often but knew almost nothing about.

In fact I hardly knew where Corney Fell was.

But looking for a place beginning with C gave me all the excuse I needed to find out.

All I knew about Corney Fell, apart from the fact that it was somewhere in the part of West Cumbria into which I had rarely ventured, was that it was almost without fail the first road to be closed when it snowed.

The words 'The Corney Fell Road' are trotted out so often by presenters on BBC Radio Cumbria that I had almost begun to imagine they had morphed into just one – 'thecorneyfellroad is closed to all traffic' being the first thing I heard when I turned on my radio after a night of moderately bad winter weather.

So where exactly, I asked myself, is it?

Well, I now know it is the little road that leads from the isolated west coast in a south-easterly direction across several miles of wild open moorland to the more populated areas of the Furness peninsular and the northern tip of Lancashire.

It is not the most accessible place.

Indeed, it took a 65 mile drive – through Carlisle, down to Whitehaven and keep on going – to get anywhere near it, by which time I was ready for the cup of tea I had decided I would seek out in the village of Ravenglass.

Ravenglass is a lovely destination in its own right – the embarkation station of the Ravenglass and Eskdale Railway for one thing, and having the wonderful Muncaster Castle just up the road for another – but for me on this occasion it was just a place with the last cafe I would see before I set off into the hills.

As I wandered its narrow streets I was amused by the realisation that Ravenglass to the Corney Fell Road was what Base Camp was to the climbers about to risk their lives on the final ascent of Everest.

I had a hasty tea in a happy little cafe beside the road leading to the station, but found myself unable to settle there with the prospect of, I hoped, somewhere much more exciting just down the road.

The Corney Hill road was all I expected it to be – rising sharply from the lowlands of the coast, past some pretty gardens and a few houses and, within just a couple of miles, turning into a wild and wonderful snake that slithered its way unconvincingly across mile after mile of the sort of countryside that leaves you marvelling at the skill of the engineers who first had the idea of building a road across such a place.

I drove on slowly, savouring the peace and the views, making mental notes of all the parking places in which a man with a Bongo might enjoy spending the night, until the road seemed to run out of steam and sank without warning into the valley beyond.

There I stopped, did a nifty three-point-turn and headed back the way I had come.

I reckoned the best Bongo spot was one of the first I had passed – just at the top of the first hill, where I could park safely on a piece of level ground with my wheels facing the sea, which I could see shining bright blue in the distance.

This was a place that satisfied all the rules I set myself for a Bongo Night.

There was no house, and no other campervan, anywhere to be seen.

I was not blocking any gateways or inconveniencing anyone by being there.

There was space just for me, so there was no danger of anyone else parking near me.

And I was able to park with my front wheels facing outwards, so I could make a hasty exit if I had to.

It was a perfect spot and I spent many minutes sitting there, enjoying having no one and nothing for company except the skylarks that filled the sky with their song as they soared and swooped above me.

And then a car went past at a speed that created a wooomph of air that made the Bongo rock.

And then another.

And another.

And then I realised that the reason my friends at Radio Cumbria make such a song and dance of the Corney Fell road being closed by snow was that it was the route favoured by hundreds of workers on the rat run to the huge Sellafield nuclear reprocessing plant a handful of miles up the coast.

Now, I had experience of Sellafield workers on a previous Bongo Night.

That was a few years before, when I had chosen to drive on another of their rat runs as I made my way to a night in the western fells.

It was my misfortune that on that occasion I had chosen to use the road at the very moment many hundreds of Sellafield workers were knocking off after a day's work, believing, it appeared, that they owned the road along which I was driving.

My route that day took me along a narrow country road which skirted the mountains between Ennerdale Bridge and the coast and which just happened to be the one used by most of the Sellafield workforce on their way home.

I met the first of them just after Ennerdale Bridge, and over the next five miles there were (and I'm not exaggerating) more than a hundred others.

Every one of them was driving too fast. Every one of them – mostly middle-aged men in ties and well-pressed shirts – passed me without acknowledgement or any sign that they were even aware that I had pulled onto the verge to get out of their way. And every one of them got my back up.

The sensible thing, I suppose, would have been for me to pull into a lay-by, make a cup of tea and calmly admire the view while this selfish convoy of arrogance made its way home.

But instead, after the first few dozen had passed, I had had enough.

No more pulling into a passing place as soon as I spotted them coming in the distance. From then on I was going to remind them that I had as much right to be on that road as they did.

My leisurely drive along that lovely road became a pointless – and, I admit, childish – game of chicken, seeing who had the courage (or bloody-mindedness, anyway) to give way last. It's true that I almost always lost, but at least I had the satisfaction of making them slow down.

And it was only towards the end, after I had pulled into a farm gateway to make way for a little blue Toyota, that a driver lifted a hand and smiled 'Thank you' as she passed.

She was a young woman, with cropped blonde hair and a huge stud in her nose, and I was so surprised by her good manners that I wanted to get out and kiss her.

If I had taken the trouble to look up the Corney Fell Road on the internet I would have known that it would be every bit as bad as that road from Ennerdale Bridge.

Just a quick Google search would have told me that it is known for two things – its sheer beauty as it sweeps over the wild country of the southern fells . . . and the speed at which cars are driven over it.

I would have found a letter to a local newspaper from a Mrs Shirley Jordan objecting to plans to introduce a speed limit on what she described as this 'higher than sea level cart track'.

In a magnificent dissection of the 'mad-heads of Sellafield' she wrote: 'If they wish to travel over Corney Fell and put their own lives at risk, let them. The world would be a lot safer without such mindless idiots.'

An online guide to a walk over the fells which included a short stretch of the Corney Fell Road included this warning: 'Normally this would be a pleasant walk but it is used as one of the main access routes by commuters to the Sellafield reprocessing site. The constant line of traffic was travelling the same direction as me and hardly any slowed down or moved over to pass at a safe distance.'

Now, perched in my eyrie above the sea, parked safely well off the road that these people believed they were entitled to be careering down, I vowed that in future I would do a little more research into the lesser known places in which I was planning to park.

It took almost an hour for the procession to pass – a high speed cavalcade of the sort of people with whom, I knew, I would be reluctant to get into a conversation in a pub – and I was relieved to find that as the revving engine of the last car faded into the distance the skylarks were still singing defiantly above my head.

I got out of the Bongo (until then I had been sitting, nursing my annoyance, in the driver's seat), unfolded a picnic chair and sat enjoying the tranquillity and gazing, without thought, at the distant sea.

I believed – rightly, as I discovered later – that I caught a glimpse of the Isle of Man . . . and maybe even the hills of North Wales and the remoter, most western parts of Scotland.

It was probably the finest view I had ever had from a Bongo parking place.

I did not see or hear another car until next morning, just as the dawn light was breaking the darkness, when the Sellafield workers – some of them thinking it was amusing to sound their horns as they passed – launched their attack once again, this time in the opposite direction.

My night on the Corney Fell road was one of the most beautiful – and most irritating – of all Bongo Nights.

But it came with an unexpected bonus.

For instead of driving back the way I had come I decided to continue on the fell road, down the hill and past where I had turned round the night before and on into a part of the country with which I was even less familiar – the place known (depending, as we shall see, on your point of view) as either the Duddon Valley or Dunnerdale.

I made an instant decision that my next Bongo Night would be spent there.

4

Dunnerdale

Having accidentally discovered a wonderful part of my home county that I had not visited before, I was keen to return there for a Bongo Night as soon as I could.

After Ambleside, Buttermere and Corney Fell, how lucky I was that I was now looking for somewhere beginning with D – and Dunnerdale, the place I had so recently fallen in love with, would do nicely

And it mattered not that many people when I spoke of Dunnerdale replied : 'Ah yes, that's the Duddon Valley, isn't it?'

I didn't care whether the place I planned to visit was Dunnerdale or Duddon – both happily began with D and were therefore equally suitable.

By the time I reached the head of the valley, after a breathtaking drive over the Wrynose Pass, I realised I was smiling.

This is a drive that puts the fun back into driving.

It is listed on the Dangerous Roads website as one of the world's most spectacular roads, and spectacular it certainly is – especially when tackled in a 23-year-old campervan.

As that website puts it: 'You need to be a confident driver to attempt this. It's one of the most spectacular climbs in England . . . a series of hairpin bends that can be unnerving for drivers. The road is single-track and narrow in places with unforgiving dry stone walls. Rising steadily to start with, after a section with a good view ahead the first, more serious inclines appear. The road becomes especially dangerous for the brakes on a couple of particularly steep turns and it's one of the most challenging sections of road in England.'

The Bongo is a vehicle that comes into its own on such roads.

While it would be foolhardy to attempt such a drive in anything bigger or less reliable, the Bongo seems to positively relish the challenge, and I like to think that it too was grinning stupidly when it reached the top.

It was tempting to continue on to the even more exciting Hardknott Pass, but I had Dunnerdale in my sights and that was down a narrow road to the left.

I knew there were two places worth visiting in the tiny village of Seathwaite-in-Dunnerdale – the church and the pub.

Even though Seathwaite Church dates back to the first half of the 16th Century it probably would not attract much attention were it not for William Wordsworth, who seems to have had a bit of a thing about the place.

Wordsworth was utterly fascinated by the River Duddon – so much so that he visited the area often, tramping for miles over the hills from his home in Grasmere and writing an astonishing 34 sonnets about it. In doing so he turned the local vicar – one Reverend Robert Walker – into even more of a legend than he probably deserved to be.

Walker was the vicar at Holy Trinity Church for 66 years in the 18th century, and was famed not just for his long ministry but also his commitment to the community and his eagerness for hard work.

Among the several other jobs he needed to do to augment his meagre £20 a year stipend – he was also a teacher, farmer, yarn-maker, beer-seller and furniture-maker (one of his bobbin chairs is still on display at Keswick museum).

Walker, who somehow also found time to father ten children, is immortalised not only in Wordsworth's poems, but also on a stone alongside a sundial outside the church, which celebrates his nickname of 'Wonderful Walker' – a title bestowed upon him, apparently, because of his many good works.

I guessed that at that time of the evening the church was unlikely to be open, and that was all the excuse I needed to head straight for the pub instead.

It was chaos – so full of people I had to shoulder charge several of them even to get a glimpse of the bar (I discovered later that most of them were staying in the campsite just up the road, ready for some fell racing event taking place the next day).

I found my way to the bar and, after checking the hand pumps of several real ales, settled for a pint of Tirril Academy 'darker' ale – not least because Tirril is the village on the northern fringe of the Lake District in which my younger son lives.

'You can't have that one – it's meaningless,' I was told by a jolly woman who stepped back to allow me more space.

'Eh?'

'A darker ale, it says,' she told me. 'Darker than what? It doesn't say. Darker than water? Darker than pale ale? Darker than Guinness? They can't just say it's darker without saying what it's darker than. It's ridiculous.'

'Blimey – I thought I was pedantic!' I said.

'Not as pedantic as her,' said a sombre faced man who later turned out to be her husband.

And so began a happy couple of hours in the company of Anne and John, and some of their friends who, unlike most of the people in the pub, all lived locally and made it very clear they considered themselves lucky to do so.

Anne told me she had been born in the village and had grown up there, though she had moved away in her youth and had returned to it only six years before.

'What about them over there?' I said, nodding my head discreetly in the direction of two middle aged couples eating at a table. 'Are they local too?'

'No, they just think they are,' she replied, before launching into a vivid description of 'people from London' who buy local houses at 'ridiculous prices' and call themselves 'local' on the strength of the two weeks every year that they spend living in them.

I told them I was on the fourth chapter of a book in which I would be taking my ancient campervan through the Lake District, staying in places A to Z.

'I've done A, B and C so now I've come here to Dunnerdale,' I said.

'No you haven't,' said Anne.

'Indeed you haven't,' her friends chorused.

Now, I didn't feel like getting into an argument with a group of locals, especially when they were as friendly and welcoming as Anne and her chums, but I felt relatively sure of my facts.

'But Dunnerdale is what it says on the signpost, and on the map,' I said. 'Both say this village is Seathwaite -in-Dunnerdale.'

'Yes, but they're wrong. It's not.'

'But . . . '

'I should know, I was born here,' said Anne with a huge grin lighting up her face.

'And she's right,' said her friends. 'This is the Duddon Valley.'

The tale of what is and what is not Dunnerdale kept us busy in enjoyable conversation for almost the whole hour it took my macaroni cheese to arrive.

It seemed (if I understood a rather confusing explanation correctly) that, strictly speaking, Seathwaite is in the Duddon Valley.

The village stands on Tarn Beck, a tributary which joins the River Duddon a short walk downstream from the pub in which we were sitting.

Dunnerdale, on the other hand, takes its name from Dunnerdale Beck, a small river I would find 'up a wiggly waggly road' over the hill to the next valley which, it seemed, only the locals knew existed.

It was only some council bureaucrat who had decided, wrongly, that the names Dunnerdale and the Duddon Valley should be interchangeable.

My new local Seathwaite friends acknowledged that even without the nameless civil servant they had another opponent (or was it ally? By now I was too confused to tell) of some influence: Alfred Wainwright, the doyen of all Cumbrian walkers, whose guidebooks are still relied upon by thousands of his earnest disciples as they tramp the fells.

'I am aware that the Duddon Valley is also properly known as Dunnerdale, a name I haven't used in the book, preferring the former,' he wrote in his book on the Southern Fells. 'It's a matter of personal choice.'

'Wainwright knew fuck all,' was how my friends in the pub summed up his expertise on the subject.

'Well, it doesn't matter very much to me – Duddon Valley and Dunnerdale both, fortunately, begin with D,' I told them. 'So as long as I spend the night somewhere around here, I'll be OK. Duddon Valley or Dunnerdale – either one will do.'

'No it won't,' said Anne. 'You came here looking for Dunnerdale so it's to Dunnerdale you should go.'

She told me that if I drove a couple more miles I'd find a turning to the left, which would take me – on the 'wiggly waggly' road she had already described – up a hill, over two cattle grids ('If you reach the gate you've gone too far') and on to a piece of open fell which would be perfect for anyone wanting to park a campervan overnight.

'And you'll be in Dunnerdale,' she said firmly.

'Not the Duddon Valley?' I asked.

'Definitely not.'

The road leading to Dunnerdale was just as wiggly waggly as Anne had described, rising sharply after a relatively flat stretch, taking me up into the wild country beneath the rocky conical peak of Stickle Pike. As I reached the brow of the hill, it was exactly as my new friends had described it – a quite spacious gravelly plateau of land beside the road, big enough for several cars, before it plunged down into an altogether darker and more mysterious landscape where the valley which contained Dunnerdale Beck stretched out below me.

I shy away from spacious parking areas these days though.

After an unfortunate experience above the Yorkshire town of Holmfirth, where I settled down in an expansive lay-by, only for it to be taken over later on by a dozen cars from the local dogging community, I have preferred to spend my nights in parking spaces too small to share with any other vehicles which may be full of people intent on watching each other having sex.

So I turned my back on the hilltop layby and drove a hundred yards back down the hill, to a small level patch of grass just big enough for me to reverse into and get the Bongo's bonnet off the road. It was a perfect site – firm and level, with wonderful views in front and to the left and right, and an enticing track leading away behind and up to a rocky outcrop which was just demanding to be climbed.

The sun was setting in the west, casting a deep red light over the hills that looked down upon what truly must have been, without argument even from my friends in the pub, either the Duddon Valley or Dunnerdale.

A few sheep wandered down to investigate, but wandered off once they found I was not as interesting as the heather they had been munching on; a handful of swifts swooped and circled above me, making the most of the last hour of summer daylight; and I sat on a rock, playing my guitar, but gently for fear of disturbing the peacefulness of it all.

This was one of the most perfect of all Bongo spots.

And I did not see another human being for nearly 12 hours.

5
Eycott Hill

Even though I was born in Devon, grew up in Somerset and still talk with a hint of a westcountry accent, I am pleased and proud to have spent the past 30 years in a county as uniquely beautiful as Cumbria.

I am not and never will be a true Cumbrian, but I love its breathtaking natural beauty, its way of life, its pace of life and the opportunities it has given – and still gives – me and my family to spend our lives doing things we would never have been able to do in any other part of the country.

Although we fly other county's flags on special occasions (Devon's on my birthday, Somerset's on our wedding anniversary) it is the flag of my adopted home that flutters most often from the flagpole on top of the hill in our garden.

The Cumbrian flag was always a bit of a mystery to me – the blue and white wavy lines across the bottom, and the green across the top were fairly obviously some graphic designer's representation of the lakes and mountains.

But what on earth was the meaning of the three star-shaped white flowers across the middle?

I eventually found out that these were signified the county flower, the Grass of Parnassus, a rare plant that grows in the Lake District and only a very few other parts of the world – mostly arctic and alpine habitats and swamps and wet forests.

I have no idea who decreed that this should be our county flower, or what perks such a decision brings with it, but if Lancashire can have a red rose and Yorkshire a white one, why should we not have a strange little plant that most people have never even heard of let alone seen?

One of the few places it can be seen is at Eycott Hill, a wonderful place that's missed by almost everyone as they hurryscurry down the A66 leading from the M6 motorway into the depths of the Lake District.

Eycott Hill only makes it into my A-Z guide by a few inches, it's true.

The eastern boundary of the Lake District National Park runs along the edge of the road that passes it, so the road itself is technically outside the National Park, and therefore – under the rules I set myself – not somewhere that qualifies for a place in my A-Z.

It was only after pulling off the road and into a little parking place beside it, that I found myself – just – inside the National Park and so able to include this little gem as the E in my alphabetical adventure.

Eycott Hill is a place I would never even have heard of had my wife Tricia not been such a keen environmentalist.

In 2015 she saw that the Cumbria Wildlife Trust – an organisation dedicated to protecting the best bits of our landscape and every living thing that makes its home within it – had launched an appeal to buy a place called Eycott Hill and the small area of wild moorland and rough meadows around it, all of which for a whole host of reasons is designated a Site of Special Scientific Interest.

Tricia gave a donation to the appeal fund, the land was successfully purchased and ever since we have felt that we own a little bit of it.

Now the Eycott Hill Nature Reserve ('a peaceful upland with spectacular views, the perfect place for a low level walk, family picnic, or wildlife adventure,' is how the Trust describes it) is one of our favourite places to go for a short unchallenging walk in stupendous scenery.

Its car park is neatly tucked away behind a low wall and many people are content to go there, sit in their cars to admire the view for a while, and then drive off without ever getting out.

It would be an ideal place to spend a night in a campervan – though perhaps not quite as ideal as the spot that I chose – a big layby just up the road, which is just a bit wilder and less well-kept, and so gives off less of a feeling that your presence overnight might not be fully appreciated.

Eycott Hill is a place that demands to be walked in – and there is no better time than in the evening, when long shadows emphasise the beauty of the landscape as the sun falls over the fells to the west.

It is a wonderful place to walk at dusk, a wonderful place to walk at dawn and a wonderful place in which to sleep in between.

This time I was not alone. Tricia – loving Eycott Hill as much as I do, and owning a few blades of grass of it – wanted to come with me.

And so did my friend Eddie (who has a campervan of his own, and several years ago had the dubious distinction of teaching me to fly a glider).

When he heard where we were going he invited himself to come too.

'That's where my family come from,' he said. 'So it'll be like going home.'

And so it was that four of us – Eddie, whose family had farmed there for generations, and whose grandfather had been born just down the road in Eycott Farm, his wife Pat, my wife Tricia and me – found ourselves back walking at Eycott Hill.

I am not expert enough to identify more than a few of the wildflowers growing like a carpet under my feet (I would not be able to tell a wood anemone from a mountain pansy, or a common butterwort from a devil's bit scabious) but you don't need to be an expert in anything to enjoy this place.

The feeling of being there was enough – the birds of prey soaring above my head, the magical calling of birds like lapwing, curlew and skylark, the dragonflies and butterflies . . . and yes, the mass of wildflowers and the huge variety of sedge and sphagnum moss. too, all added up to creating a very special place.

But all of that – the flowers, the birds, the insects, the rocks that tell the tale of the lava that flowed there from the volcanoes of 460 million years ago – was, to me, just the warm-up act for the true star.

The greatest, most awe-inspiring part of the Eycott Hill nature reserve was the hill itself.

A weird funny-shaped, rocky promontory – a mere 345 metres high – which looks out towards the biggest of the mountains affords what I reckon is the best and most complete view of anywhere in the Lake District.

We paused on the top for a hot drink and a biscuit (Cornish fairings that I had baked the day before, in honour of the far western roots that both Pat and I enjoy) and looked around us for our next challenge.

I had seen that the Lake District National Park Authority had only recently established a new right of way, leading to Eycott Hill from Mungrisdale – a village whose haphazard pattern of roofs and chimneys was ahead of us to the west – and I was determined to give it a try.

Such a path, if we could find it, would open up a circular six-mile route that had not been possible before – from the little car park, westwards to the hill, then on the new path further west to Mungrisdale, then north along the road for half a mile turning east along an old established track that would bring us back almost to where we had started.

The only problem was that there was no path to be seen from our vantage point of top of Eycott Hill.

But eventually we spotted a post – and then another – with its tip painted white, giving a clue that it might just be some sort of marker to a path hidden in the undergrowth.

We walked (stumbled might be a better word, such was the roughness of the ground beneath our feet) to the first, and then to the second. And then to the third and fourth, as they too came into view.

And that is the problem with new rights of way. Getting them recognised, and legally established under the law, is one thing; getting them to look like footpaths, beaten down by hundreds of passing feet is something else – something that clearly had not yet been achieved.

Still, we marched on, the four of us – possibly the first people ever to have walked the route – going from one white-topped post to the next, beating a way through the shrubs and tall grasses and leaving in our wake the beginnings of what one day might become an obvious footpath.

Two smart and sturdy wooden footbridges, still clean and bright and displaying not a sign of the moss and lichen that would come with age, took the path over the rivers that, though small, would have posed too big an obstacle to the average walker.

To my surprise the streams were flowing towards the south, though I knew that the River Caldew, not half a mile away would be flowing north towards Carlisle and Solway Firth.

It was Eddie who put me right.

The water here was heading not to the Caldew, but to the gloriously named Glenderamackin, which would eventually join the Greta, then the Derwent and on into the North Sea at Workington.

'That must be the watershed,' he said, pointing to an area of scrub – only slightly higher than the ground on which we were standing – to our right.

An hour later, while enjoying a picnic on a welcome bench beside the Glenderamackin where it tumbled through Mungrisdale village, Tricia delivered her verdict.

'This is a gorgeous walk,' she said. 'Well done for finding it.'

And she began making plans to come back with her friends from the Geltsdale Fellwalkers, a group of keen women walkers always on the look-out for somewhere new to explore.

'The ladies will love it,' she said. 'It's just their cup of tea.'

We left the relative comfort of the riverside bench and headed north along the road, veering off only when a fingerpost pointed to Murrah – a small community in which some more of Eddie's farming ancestors had once lived, and the place we knew we had to pass through on our way back to the car park.

Within a few minutes we realised that the path (or lack of it) bore no relation either to what the signpost had told us or to what we could see on our Ordnance Survey map.

Instead we found ourselves in a small and obviously ancient wood growing out of what can be described as nothing other than a bog.

We might have lost the path, but we had found the watershed – a piece of land left sodden by a maze of little rivulets as they wandered this way and that as if trying to make up their minds whether to head north to Carlisle or west to Workington.

The watershed was right under our boots (something I found strangely exciting, since I had never knowingly stood on a watershed before) and, after I took a few more squelchy steps into a puddle that was deeper than it looked, it was actually inside them.

We headed for a ramshackle wooden bridge (which was not where the map told us it should be), and a rudimentary stile and – eventually – the merest suggestion of a footpath so indistinct that it might not have been used since the days when Eddie's relatives last walked it on their way to the pub in Mungrisdale in about 1892.

The path, such as it was, was so muddy and ankle-breakingly uneven it was impossible to walk in a straight line and we had to leap from one dry patch to another as if engaged in some weird form of rural hopscotch.

'Forget what I was saying about bringing the ladies here,' Tricia said as she stretched a leg to reach a safe-looking dry tussock among the quagmire. 'It's not their sort of thing at all.'

6
Far Sawrey

There is a corner of the Lake District that's probably better known to the Japanese than it is to the average British tourist. A few miles south of Ambleside, and nestling among the pretty hills on the western side of Windermere, is the farm where Beatrix Potter lived for most of her adult life.

Now, I have no great interest in Beatrix Potter, apart from being grateful for the great work she did in protecting the Lake District environment that I enjoy so much these days. I have, as far as I can remember, never read any of her books – having trouble, even as a small child, with the concept of a rabbit that talks and wears a blue jacket – but the Japanese are obsessed with them.

It seems they use the books to learn their English (for them 'The Tale of Peter Rabbit' is virtually a school textbook) and when they grow up they feel compelled to visit the places in which the stories are set. Which, according to my friends in the tourist industry, is why in any queue for any attraction in any part of the Lake District you are likely to be standing behind, in front of or beside (or, in the high season, probably all three) a group of young Japanese people clutching books with pictures of fluffy bunnies on the cover.

Such considerations were far from my mind though when, while scouring the atlas for a Bongo Night spot beginning with F, my eye I settled on a village Far Sawrey.

Far Sawrey is one of a pair of villages – the other, unsurprisingly called Near Sawrey, is less than a mile away – which are famous for their links with Beatrix Potter.

Near Sawrey is where Beatrix lived, wrote her books, painted her pictures and eventually died and she used a number of sites in the villages in books such as 'The Tale of Tom Kitten', 'The Fairy Caravan' and 'The Tale of Jemima Puddle-Duck'.

Although she wrote them when she was back home with her parents in London, Potter's early stories were inspired by her annual holidays in the Lake District, and she used the royalties from those first books to buy Hill Top farm in 1905.

Four years later she bought the farm opposite too, and that became her main Lakeland base and the one she used for most of her work.

She bought many more pieces of land and property in and around Sawrey, becoming a prominent member of the farming community, and by the time she died in 1943 she owned 14 farms and 4,000 acres of land, all of which she left to the National Trust.

Whether she would have approved of someone parking a campervan for an overnight stay on her land is of course debatable.

But Far Sawrey is where I headed – not just because it began with F and there seemed a good chance of finding somewhere to park there, but also because within a few miles were two other Fs – Finsthwaite and Force Forge – which looked like providing acceptable alternatives in case of emergency.

It was only after I reached the Windermere shore at Far Sawrey that I realised I had been there before – on my walk beside the lake after the first of my A-Z Bongo Nights, on the hill above Ambleside.

Far Sawrey was, though I had not grasped the fact until then, where I had caught the passenger ferry across the lake to Bowness-on-Windermere.

So on that day I must have walked past the very spot in which now I was hoping to spend the night.

The trouble was that the lake shore from Far Sawrey northwards is quite some magnet to visitors, and by the time I got there all the potential Bongo Night places were already full of cars and, yes, campervans of the enormous motorhome variety.

I could see that there were several spots in which I would be happy to spend the night, and though there were a few low-key 'No camping' signs fixed to the fence alongside the road to deter people from pitching tents in what would otherwise have been a champion camping field, there was nothing stopping me parking a campervan beside the lake if only I could have found the space to do so.

It was still early in the evening so I switched to plan B . . . and set off towards Finsthwaite in the hope that I might find a more lonely place there.

After just a few minutes a succession of narrow lanes brought me out down a sharp hill, towards a Give Way sign at a junction with a road which was only slightly wider.

As I pulled to a cautious stop a police motor cycle passed along that mainer road, with its blue lights flashing. Then two more, weaving from side to side, and then a shining black limousine.

'Prince Charles!' I said to myself, remembering that I had heard a radio report of his being in Cumbria that day to, among other things, stir a vat of chutney at the Hawkshead Relish factory.

As he passed in front of me I saw that, though he had the three motorbike outriders in front of him, he had none behind.

So I pulled out smartly and followed.

It appealed greatly to my sense of the ridiculous.

A convoy headed by three police motorcycles, blue lights flashing, with the heir to the throne in his gleaming limo . . . being pursued by a pensioner in a rusting 23-year-old Bongo.

As we made our way at a speed that would otherwise have been excessive through the Cumbrian countryside I waved and smiled at the drivers of the oncoming cars who the police had made to stop, and I liked to think Charles was doing the same.

I just wished he would turn round and look out of his back window and give me a wave as well.

He didn't, of course,

And I lost him when I turned right into Finsthwaite village and he went straight on to progress towards (presumably) Lancaster, where a train would be waiting to speed him home.

Which left me time to discover that Finsthwaite was no place for a man to spend a night in his Bongo.

Indeed, charming village though it no doubt was, it had nowhere to park and the only thing to commend it was that its name began with an F.

Force Forge, a few miles on, was not much better. Just a straggle of farms and houses and, on the far side, a couple of rough lay-bys which would have served in an emergency. So it looked like I had no real alternative but to continue back to Far Sawrey to see if any of the better parking places there had been vacated.

As I turned left, back along the road that leads alongside the lake, I saw that things had changed in the couple of hours I had been away.

Most of the cars had now gone and even the biggest motorhome, which I had thought was parked there for the night, was now noticeable only by its absence and the empty space in the parking place where it had been.

I did a quick U-turn and parked in its place, at the top of a gravelly pull-in which fell in a gentle slope to form a pebbly beach upon which the waters of Windermere were quietly lapping in a whispering breeze.

It was an idyllic scene. The water blue in the early evening sunshine, a dozen white boats bobbing at their moorings, the green hills on the far side of the lake becoming ever more shadowy as the sun went down behind me . . .

As perfect a Bongo spot as I was ever likely to find.

And then I saw, easing gently into view from behind the trees on my right, the unmistakeable outline of the Windermere car ferry.

This was something of a surprise because I knew that the ferry had been out of action for months – first after 80 people had had to be evacuated from it after it caught fire, and then because of what was described as 'routine maintenance' – and I had not heard that it was back in service.

A quick look at the local newspaper's website on my mobile put me straight: The ferry, which cuts out a tedious 14-mile drive around the southern tip of Windermere, had completed its safety trials and, that day, would be running a couple of trips in the evening before resuming full service the next day.

'Perfect,' I thought. 'That sorts out how I will be getting home.'

For now though, a walk along the lake beckoned.

Although the lakeside path had left me rather underwhelmed when I had walked it after my Ambleside Bongo Night, it seemed a good, if unadventurous, bet now.

I set off heading north, towards where I had witnessed the canine arse-wiping episode on my previous visit, but quickly realised what I wanted was something rather more satisfying than an unchallenging there-and-back stroll, so I looked out for any sign of an alternative path.

It came after a few hundred yards, a signpost pointing to my left, up a rough path that seemed to lead through the rocks and the trees in a direction which, I guessed, would take me sufficiently far 'inland' to reach the Far Sawrey.

It took me about an hour's strenuous walking to reach the village – and, more importantly, its pub, The Cuckoo Brow Inn – and by the time I got there, I confess, I was well ready for a pint.

I gauged I was the only tourist in the pub. A barmaid who asked if I was 'local' but did not seem especially interested in the answer, a couple of clusters of well-dressed locals who did not bother to spare me a glance as I made my way to a chair in the window . . . and that was about it.

I downed my beer but did not feel sufficiently welcome to bother with the food that I had been half-hoping would be impossible to resist. Instead I headed for the door, keen to make the most of the remaining daylight so I could find my way on a different footpath back to the Bongo.

The path took me past a handful of pretty cottages, downhill through a field and past a small nature reserve to the lake shore and back to the Bongo for a supper made up of various salads that I had bought at a delicatessen in Penrith earlier in the day.

It got dark quickly and I finished my meal by the light of a small battery powered lantern that has accompanied me without ever dimming on all my Bongo adventures (the van has its own interior lighting, of course, but, perhaps unnecessarily, I am always wary of relying on it for fear of flattening the battery).

Afterwards I read a few pages of a book ('Eminence' by Morris West – an author I met very early in my career as a journalist) but found my heart was not really in it; then I played a few tunes on my guitar, but found my heart wasn't in that either, so I made up the bed, turned the radio on and fell asleep to Hollywood 'screen siren' Kathleen Turner (someone else I interviewed many years ago) talking about 'the enduring mystique of the femme fatale'.

7

Gowbarrow

There are several reasons why Ullswater is my favourite of the Cumbrian lakes. It is, to my mind anyway, the most scenically beautiful of them all; it is the closest to where I live; it is where my wife Tricia and I have spent some of our happiest times exploring in our kayaks; it has the best tourist boats (its famous 'steamers' are not really steamers at all since their old engines have long ago been replaced by modern diesel ones, but with their smart green hulls and red funnels they really look the part, which is probably all that matters); and – for the benefit of this Bongo Night – it has along its western shore three places whose names all begin with G.

Glenridding, Glencoyne and Gowbarrow . . . and all three have some very attractive places right beside the lake in which a Bongo could be parked for the night.

Top of my list was the National Trust car park at Glencoyne, a place I know very well because it makes an excellent place from which Tricia and I can launch the boats we bought a couple of years ago.

Tricia had had an ancient two-person Canadian canoe for some time and we had had some great times in it paddling around some of the lesser known nooks and crannies of the lakes.

But I never felt entirely comfortable in it (Tricia would tell you it was because I, sitting in the front, was not enough of a team player to accept taking orders from her as she sat in the captain's seat at the back – not for nothing is the Canadian canoe labelled the 'divorce boat') and there were even times when I felt positively unsafe.

It was also incredibly heavy, so that it required a real effort for us to lift it on and off the roof bars on our car before and after every voyage.

And – its final death knell – it developed a crack, almost a hole, presumably after we hit a jagged rock during one of our more enthusiastic landings, and though it would probably have been serviceable for a few more years yet, since it was not actually letting in water, a crack in a canoe in which I had never felt entirely safe was enough to encourage us to think about getting something else.

The solution came when we encountered a group of teenagers using a type of kayak we had never paid much attention to until then.

Small, tough, manoeuvrable, virtually uncapsizable . . . and big enough only for one person, so if we bought two we could each be masters of our own ship.

Within a couple of weeks Tricia had bought a pink and purple one, I had bought a yellow and orange one and we were off across the lakes in a splashing kaleidoscope of colour.

Glencoyne, with its level and spacious car park just across from a handy pebbly beach at the waterside, was an ideal place from which to launch our new canoes.

And now it was an almost ideal place in which to park the van on my seventh Bongo Night.

I had a vague plan of how to spend my day, so I packed up my rucsac with a few essentials – a map, a bottle of water, a cagoule, a camera and, just in case it should turn cold, a sweater – and headed north along a gravel footpath recently installed by the owners of Ullswater Steamers to link the village of Glenridding (where they have their headquarters and one of their main piers) with Aira Force, the National Trust beauty spot where they have built a new jetty three miles north.

The path is now part of the Ullswater Way, a 20-mile walking route that, as its name implies, goes all the way round my favourite lake – too far for me or any other normal person to manage in one day, but easy enough if broken up into three or four separate sections.

My section, on this day, stretched less than two miles and though I sat on every available rock and fallen tree to soak up the view and took every opportunity to dawdle, I was at Aira Force in no time.

It was, as is usual in high summer, packed. People thronged around the little café just inside the gate, drivers cruised in vain around the car park looking for a space, and families in unsuitable shoes set off along the footpaths in the hope of being able to reach the waterfall from which the area gets in name.

I was in the mood for more of a walk than I had already had, so I headed across the car park and along a path that was being ignored by almost everyone else.

Aira Force is, even when it is swamped by tourists, and even when there has been so little rain the word 'force' is a bit of an exaggeration when it comes to describing the waterfall, a wonderful place for a walk that's hard enough to make you puff but easy enough to leave you with enough energy to do something else afterwards.

So I climbed up to the pretty little stone bridge that crosses Aira Beck as it tumbles down from the mountains above, which is where most people pause to take their selfies before walking back down the other side to their cars.

I pressed on further up the hill to the two lesser visited, but on this day no more impressive waterfalls known with similar exaggeration as High Force and High Cascades – and found I had enough of the place to myself to find a rock to sit on and enjoy the tranquillity before zigzagging back down the paths to the car park.

By now I knew what I was going to do . . . if I could.

A timetable pinned on the wall of a building labelled 'Information' told me that if I hung around for just over an hour I could catch the last steamer of the day from the new jetty across the road.

That would take me to Pooley Bridge, at the northern end of the lake – about five miles from where I had left the Bongo.

My only question was whether I would then be able to catch a bus back to where I wanted to be.

There was no bus timetable pinned on the wall and I had no confidence that, though she demonstrated an eager friendliness in the way she sold her ice creams, the girl assistant at the information counter would be able to help (not least because she did not look very much older than my grand-daughter, who had just turned 13).

Not for the first time in my life I was reminded not to jump to conclusions.

'Do you know when the last bus from Pooley Bridge back to Glenridding is?' I asked with no hope at all.

'Let me just check,' she said, with the sort of smile that made me wish briefly that I was 50 years younger.

She opened a drawer in the desk in front of her, picked out a small folded piece of paper and smiled at me again.

'It's at 5.57 – call it six o'clock because it's usually a little bit late,' she told me. 'So if you're catching the steamer you would have more than ten minutes to spare.'

'How did you know?' I asked, but she just smiled and told me to have a good trip.

I wandered down to the jetty and sat on a rock on the beach (sitting on a rock was becoming something of a feature of the day) to await the steamer.

The only other people there were two small boys who were paddling and skimming pebbles across the lake, watched idly by their mother.

She was, frankly a rather fearsome looking woman – of substantial proportions, with aggressive tattoos down each arm, from shoulder to wrist – but I rather liked the fact that, though both her children were in their school uniforms, she was allowing them to get the bottom of their trousers wet.

It was only when the elder one went in up to his knees that she called him back.

'Be careful,' she called out, 'I think the tide is coming in.'

She might have been joking, but I think she wasn't.

And the tattoos on her muscly arms told me she might not appreciate being told that here, on an inland lake like Ullswater, she would have to wait a very long time indeed to see the tide come in.

The steamer, when it came, was nearly empty. Indeed as I walked aboard I thought I was the only passenger on it.

'Have I got the whole boat to myself?' I asked the young deckhand.

'Not quite,' he said. 'There are four people downstairs.'

I was pleased to see him roll his eyes as he said it, as if to confirm my view that it took a special type of person to spend good money for a trip on England's most beautiful lake on one of the most perfect days of the summer and then choose to spend it confined to a cabin almost below the water line.

'That's fine – but I'm going up to the front.'

My younger son Will, who spent several years working as a deckhand on these same steamers, used to talk of the strange behaviour of some of his paying customers.

One, he told me, had to ask which side of the boat to get off ('We usually recommend the side next to the jetty, madam'); another asked how, if the compass pointed north, the captain knew which way south was.

One was determined to buy a ticket to Ambleside, just as, he said, he had done the previous year – and was not satisfied when Will tried to explain such a thing was not and never had been possible because Ambleside was on an entirely different lake and any voyage to it would see the boat having to sail over the Kirkstone Pass.

I should, therefore, have not been surprised to hear that some people chose to coop themselves up in the cabin instead of enjoying the views and fresh air out on deck.

Happy not to have any unwelcome company, I settled in the bow, spreading my arms wide on the gunwales to make the most of the sunshine.

Sitting there at the very front of the boat, with the warm breeze gently ruffling my hair as the Western Belle slowly pulled away from the jetty, I contemplated yet again how lucky I was to be living the life I was living.

Then I had another thought: I was bloody freezing. True, the sun was still shining brightly, but any warmth from it was being blown away by the coldness of the wind as the boat sped towards its end-of-the-day destination.

I had the feeling that the captain, knowing that this was the last trip of the day, was getting every ounce of speed from the engine so he could get home early and do something even more enjoyable than cruising around the Lake District in the sunshine.

I also had the feeling that maybe the four people who had chosen the cabin over the deck were maybe not such dullards after all.

The boat reached the Pooley Bridge jetty just a few minutes early, as I expected, which gave me time to walk the quarter of a mile into the village rather than stand waiting at the bus stop.

Pooley Bridge is a place I like in spite of myself. I hate the crowds of tourists, the cheap tat sold in some of the shops and the fact that it is often impossible to find a parking space, and yet . . .

Rather like Keswick, its much bigger cousin that suffers from all of the above – and more – there is something about it that's just plain fun.

And it's a village I came to admire for the way it bounced back after much of it was trashed by the floods unleashed by Storm Desmond on December 6 2015.

As I sat hunkered down by a comforting log fire on that dreadful Sunday afternoon, I listened in horror to the reports of how, for the second time in just a few years, parts of my home county were, quite literally, being washed away.

In Carlisle, just six miles from my home, more than 7,000 homes were flooded and in other parts of Cumbria houses were wrecked, schools ravaged and hotels left in ruins as more than a foot of rain fell in just one day.

But it was only when I heard that Pooley Bridge's beautiful 300-year-old stone bridge – so much a symbol of the very best of the Lake District – had been washed away that I was reduced to tears.

Today that bridge has still not been replaced by anything permanent, though a fine-looking stainless steel one is in the offing, but the village of Pooley Bridge has otherwise bounced back to a remarkable degree, thanks mainly to the sheer bloody-mindedness and hard work of the people who live there.

It is a place to which I go quite often, so after walking in from the Ullswater steamers' jetty I felt no need to stay for long.

And anyway I knew that the bus that arrived soon after six was the last one of the evening.

I love public transport – as I proved when I once travelled from the South Devon village in which I was born, all the way to Cumbria, where I now live (that was a zig-zag journey of 865 miles on 41 buses, all done for free using my old folks' bus pass), and the ride along the shore of Ullswater on the No 508 Stagecoach bus is a trip I love more than most.

Anyone arriving in the Lake District for the first time would do well to take that bus for a spectacular introduction to all that this fabulous area has to offer.

My plan had been to get off at the stop at the Glencoyne car park where I had left the Bongo, but I was enjoying it so much I decided to go past it, to carry on to Glenridding, where, I knew, I would be able to buy myself the supper that would save me having to cook something in the van.

And anyway Glenridding is another place worth visiting, for many of the same reasons as Pooley Bridge. It has the same combination of too many tourists and too many cheap souvenirs, ameliorated by some breathtaking scenery and the knowledge that here too is a community which somehow recovered from the nightmarish hell unleashed by Storm Desmond.

Glenridding was, in fact, hit twice.

After a month of heavy rain Glenridding beck eventually burst its banks on the Saturday afternoon, as people living there made frantic efforts to protect their homes.

The water, along with thousands of tonnes of silt, gravel and stone that had been carried down the fells from landslips all the way up to Helvellyn, flowed right through the heart of the village.

The village was cut off for three days – during which time a second storm sent yet more water surging through even as the rescue services were trying to start clearing up the mayhem of the first.

Roads were ripped up, houses nearly crushed, phone lines flattened, electricity cut off, water supplies – with vicious irony – were suspended and more than 20,000 tonnes of gravel and stone were dumped on Jenkins Field, beside the steamer pier, when the torrent of water at last lost its power.

Today – thanks once again to the spirit of the locals – Glenridding shows few scars from that dreadful time.

And the Glenridding Hotel, which was so badly wrecked that it could not be reopened for a year, is back . . . better than ever.

It seemed appropriate to pop across to it when my bus deposited me in the huge tourist car park after my wonderful 20-minute ride along the Ullswater shore.

The Beckside Bar – named after the stream that had caused such havoc just a few years before – was bustling with tourists, none of whom seemed to be taking any notice of the huge TV screen that dominated the area in which I found the only available table.

I tried to ignore the rolling reports of the previous night's foreign football (the English season, in which I would have been more interested, had ended some weeks previously) and concentrated instead on my pint of – because I was in Cumbria – Jennings Cumberland Ale.

I had ordered a Japanese chicken katsu curry, which at least gave me something to divert my attention for a few minutes, but in truth, after almost a whole day of being left to enjoy my own quiet company, the contrast was too great. I was in no mood for a busy pub full of noisy holidaymakers (I got the feeling that the Beckside was not much frequented by many people who might have described themselves as local).

I finished my beer and my curry more quickly than was strictly necessary, grabbed my rucsac and made for the door.

My plan now was to walk the mile or two back to the Bongo and then go for a short drive to see if I could find anywhere better – or, rather, even better – than the Glencoyne National Trust car park in which to spend the night.

It was a more interesting walk than I had anticipated – a rough and rocky path, running roughly parallel to the main road, but diving off every now and then to take in a beach, avoid a rock or pass a clump of trees.

These days it is part of the Ullswater Way, the path on which my day had started, and it attracts hundreds of people every day in summer, most of whom make use of the Ullswater Steamers' new sailings to Aira Force to make a very pleasant circular trip.

On this evening I did not see another soul . . . a situation that continued when I reached the car park and found the Bongo was the only vehicle left in it.

I would have been happy enough to spend the night there, but the National Trust car park is on the 'wrong' side of the road, too far away from the water, and I knew that within a few miles I would find a lay-by immediately alongside the lake.

The idea of being lulled to sleep by the sound of the water gently lapping on the pebbles on the beach was enough to persuade me to drive back north along the lake in search of such a place.

And there, in a place called Gowbarrow – and therefore still satisfying my criterion of being somewhere beginning with G – I found the perfect spot.

There were in fact three small lay-bys, all of which can be pretty well guaranteed to be full of cars during the day, but which on that evening were all empty, so I chose the smallest, from which on other occasions in the past Tricia and I had launched our kayaks.

The great thing about those lay-bys – apart from their proximity to the lapping waters of Ullswater – is that there is no danger of being chased away by an angry landowner who does not share my enthusiasm for campervanning.

Indeed the landowner here positively encourages overnight stays.

Sam Beaumont, of nearby Gowbarrow Hall farm, has put up notices in each lay-by, telling campervanners that they are welcome to park there . . . especially if they help him with his conservation projects by making a small donation through his crowdfunding Just Giving page.

That seems to me to be a great idea, and one that gives visitors an easy way of giving something back to help the landscape that they are there to enjoy, but I fear most people don't bother.

The last time I looked at his website I saw that in five months only nine people had made donations – and one of them was my wife, who gave £5 after we had launched our kayaks there, and another was me, who gave the suggested £10 for my Bongo Night's sleep.

Compared with the dozens of people who had parked their campervans overnight there in that time, that strikes me as a pretty disappointing response.

Still, for my £10 I got a good night's sleep – lulled to sleep by the sound of the waves on the pebbles just outside my window, just as I had hoped.

8
Honister

From the early days of my owning a campervan there was one parking spot above all others in which I wanted to spend a night: A large, level site beside a huge boulder on the lower slopes of the Honister Pass in the Lake District, just where the valley opens up after the road descends dramatically in a series of tight bends and even steeper hills once it has come over the top from Borrowdale.

Every time I passed it (which was often, since it lies in one of my favourite parts of the Lake District) I told myself: 'One day I'll be spending the night there.'

Little did I think that one day it would nearly kill me.

I knew that it would be a wonderful place to park overnight in high summer, with the red sun setting over the mountains late in the evening just before bedtime.

But I also knew it would be even better in the middle of winter, when I would wake up and pull open the curtains to see the magnificence beyond – a perfect frosty winter's morning, with the early sun adding a soft golden glow to the snow on the felltops as it rose on the mountains behind me.

And if it happened to be so cold that there were icicles in the stream as it tumbled down the valley beside me . . . so much the better!

When the weather forecasts promised bitterly cold weather, with snow on the tops, bright sunshine and only an off-chance of a brief wintry shower I knew I would never get a better opportunity.

It was dark when I got there and the sky was lit by thousands of stars, and despite the cold I got out of the Bongo, just to stand quietly, to enjoy the stillness and remoteness of such a place.

I slept well, but woke in the night, and left the Bongo for a few minutes to marvel at the scene in which I was such a small part – a scene by now illuminated by a full moon which showed me, for the first time, that there was indeed snow on the tops.

In the morning I cooked my breakfast and spent more than an hour walking around my territory in the sunshine, investigating the stream . . . and simply enjoying being there.

A few cars passed in each direction, and their drivers mostly waved in friendly (and, I liked to think, envious) fashion when they saw me.

I was planning to continue in the direction I'd been heading the night before, going on to Buttermere and then up over Newlands to Keswick, but as I sat in the driver's seat about to start the engine I noticed that the mountains ahead of me were disappearing under a white cloud so thick and so dirty only a fool would have chosen to drive into it.

I made a quick mental calculation based on the speed at which the cloud seemed to be heading towards me, and after a somewhat panicky three-point turn headed back up the hill away from it.

Above me and ahead of me now, the sun was shining; behind me it was nearly dark.

I was nearly at the top of the hill, basking in the sunshine and congratulating myself on making such a hasty exit, when the darkness caught up with me and I noticed it was snowing.

Just a little at first, a few flakes falling from an incongruously blue sky. Then a little more. Then a lot more, then a blizzard and almost before I knew it the Bongo was no longer climbing the hill – it was sliding backwards, back down the way I had come. It was out of control and slithering towards either a stone wall to my left or a sheer drop down into a ravine to my right.

Skidding backwards down a steep hill in a two-ton campervan, the driver doesn't have much choice. He simply has to sit there and await developments.

I vaguely remember shouting 'Shit!' at the top of my voice, but otherwise could merely wait and see which way the laws of gravity would take me. Into the wall or into the chasm?

If it had been the chasm the Bongo would have tumbled at least 20 feet down into the beck and I would, at best, have been severely injured.

Fortunately it was the wall.

The front of the van swung suddenly to the right, as if it had decided that there was enough room to do a 180 degree turn so it could simply drive sedately back to the bottom of the hill as if nothing had happened.

But as it did so the rear of the van hit the wall with a deep scrunch, leaving the Bongo stranded almost broadside across the road.

I got out . . . and nearly fell flat on my back. It's a cliché to say the road was like an ice rink, but the road was like an ice rink.

But I knew that anyone coming towards me at anything other than snail's pace would be unable to stop in those conditions so I had somehow to reach the top of the hill, about 50 yards ahead of me, to flag down any cars in time to stop them sliding down and crashing into the stranded Bongo.

I headed on foot up the hill with great difficulty, slipping and falling and cursing and praying that I would be in time to flag down any approaching traffic.

The first car, mercifully coming very slowly, was driven by a mountain rescue volunteer on his way to a training exercise in the valley. The second was a brand new Land-Rover containing a film crew from London who were planning to spend the day making a promotional video advertising their vehicle's prowess on difficult terrain.

We all stood around the Bongo (most of us hanging onto wing mirrors, door handles and any other protuberances that might stop us sliding on our backsides down the hill) and quickly came to the conclusion that there was nothing we could do,

The road was so slippery there was no hope of using manpower alone to shift the van, and not even the new Land-Rover would be able reverse back up the hill, towing the Bongo as it went.

The only hope was that the staff at the Honister Slate Mine at the top of the hill would be willing to bring some sort of tractor – ideally with a snowplough on the front – down the road to rescue me.

To say that I was embarrassed was putting it mildly. How many times had I sat at home in bad weather, listening to BBC Radio Cumbria reports that various passes in the Lake District were blocked – not by the snow, but by vehicles (campervans, even!) – which had proved incapable of getting through it?

And how many times had I harrumphed: 'Stupid bloody idiots! They shouldn't have been there at all in these conditions.'

The mountain rescue man was a great deal more sympathetic to me than I was myself.

'It's not your fault,' he said. 'The sun was shining when you started, so how were you to know? It could have happened to any of us. The weather can change in an instant. You were just unlucky.'

The boss of the Slate Mine said more or less the same thing when he eventually came over the horizon in a digger tractor, with a young woman assistant cheerfully shovelling salt and sand from the bucket on the front.

They gingerly brought the digger to within a few feet of the Bongo (they didn't want it sliding down the hill any more than I did) and spread extra shovelfuls of salt under my wheels. We waited and watched for a few minutes while the salt did its job and the tarmac began to emerge from under the freshly fallen snow.

The digger trundled back to the top of the hill and the mountain rescue man looked at me.

'Go on, give it a try,' he said. 'If you get going, just keep going . . . and don't stop till you get to the top.'

I started the engine and gently pressed the accelerator. The Bongo eased forwards and I cautiously turned the steering wheel to point it up the hill rather than towards the chasm.

The wheels gripped, the onlookers cheered . . . and I drove in stately fashion to the top of the hill.

In the slate mine's car park I thanked all those who'd helped – not just for their patience and their muscles, but the kind words with which they tried to convince me I was not to blame.

The whole episode lasted about two hours and it cost me a dent in the Bongo's tailgate, a smashed rear light, a badly bent bumper, £20 I put in the slate mine's charity box . . . and a whole lot of wounded pride.

Because of what happened at Honister I have always had a soft spot for the people who run the slate mine there and have silently supported their attempts to use it to provide added excitements to the many visitors who want to do something other than simple fell-walking on their visits to the Lake District.

There are those – including many of my friends – who believe that the Lake District, especially now that it is a UNESCO World Heritage Site, should be left as it is, unspoiled and uncommercialised, as they say.

There should be no place, they tell us, for man-made excitements (they cite everything from cable cars and residential house boats to tarmac cycle paths and 4x4s using ancient farm tracks) and the fells should be left undisturbed for walkers to enjoy in quiet contemplation.

Nowhere is that controversy more pronounced than at the Honister slate mine, where the owners have fought for many years to instal a zipwire.

My own view, which I accept counts for little, is that of all places in the Lake District the slate mine is best suited for such ideas.

To argue that the area should be left 'unspoiled' is to ignore the fact that it was spoiled very many years ago.

Quarrying has been going on there since the late 17th century, with underground workings stretching deep into the surrounding fells and the cliffs being scarred by the paths made for the teams of packhorses which dragged the slate away on sledges.

There have been aerial ropeways, bridges and railways for generations of quarrymen and it was only in the 1980s, when the mines ceased operating, that the place stopped being disturbed by the bustle and noise of heavy industry – in my book hardly the 'unspoiled' Lake District landscape that some people seek to portray.

In 1997 the site was reopened by Mark Weir, a local businessman who redeveloped the mining side – producing small quantities of roofing slate at the same time as introducing underground tours and a visitor centre for simple tourists and a via ferrata upon which the thrill-seeking ones could scale a challenging cliff path while clipped onto wire cables with safety harnesses.

In 2011 the via ferrata was named winner of Cumbria Tourism's 'Best Tourism Experience in the Lake District' and with Weir's dream seeming to be going well he made it known that he wanted to expand it by creating a zip wire from the top of a nearby mountain called Fleetwith Pike down to the mine below.

But then things went badly – and tragically – wrong.

First, the company faced prosecution in the courts accused of damaging a site of special scientific interest by extending the via ferrata further than his planning permission allowed.

And then on a filthy night in March 2011 the very existence of the mine and the company that owned it was put in doubt when Mark Weir was killed when the helicopter he was piloting crashed shortly after taking off from the mine.

The following year, with the company now being run by his partner, the Lake District National Park Authority refused permission for the zip wire on the grounds that it would adversely impact its surroundings – even though several local business and tourist organisations, and Cumbria's own mountaineer Sir Chris Bonington, spoke in favour of it.

It was another six years before planning permission was at last given, for a kilometre-long zip wire down the mountainside.

Even so, the very idea of the zip wire – and, apparently, of the sound of tourists screaming in excitement as they sped down it – was too much for those who think the Lake District should be open only to those willing to enjoy it on their terms, and even though it is now going ahead with all the necessary permissions there are still many people who vociferously and unceasingly complain about it.

Now I believe it is a great idea for the Lake District to be opened up to people – whole races, even – who would not traditionally go there, and I can't help feeling that an ugly old industrial site, long ago scarred by the sight and sound of mining, is a pretty good place to build something that provides the sort of thrill that can't be found in a world populated only by hearty folk in walking boots and brightly coloured cagoules.

My crash on the Honister Pass remains the scariest thing that has ever happened to me in the Bongo, but every cloud has its silver lining, even when it's preparing to dump half a ton of snow on you.

For without it I would never have encountered my friend Tim Wing – a man I met only because I was too mean to pay almost £450 (the best price I could find online) for the replacement bumper and light cluster I needed before I could take the Bongo to a bodyshop to have the dents and scrapes beaten out.

On the recommendation of a fellow member of one of the Bongo owners' groups on Facebook, I contacted Tim, who runs a specialist garage called the Bongo Barn from a renovated farm building deep in the Northumbrian hills.

He agreed to sell me a secondhand bumper, a replacement light cluster, two hub caps, an ash tray (useful for keeping loose change in) and a few other bits and pieces I spotted when I visited him . . . all for less than £100.

I was delighted with the deal, but even more pleased to meet Tim, for it is largely down to him that my ancient Bongo has survived long enough to complete this A-Z challenge.

If my brilliant local garage man Peter Allison is the reliable GP you need when you're feeling a bit under the weather, Tim is the specialist consultant you go to when things get really rough.

He is a man who lives and breathes Bongos – repairing them, servicing them, importing them and selling them – and knows so much about them that he inspires total confidence in people like me who know almost nothing at all.

After a couple of false starts (he trained as a lawyer, and as a plumber and heating engineer and was then planning to become a police officer) he has managed to turn his teenage obsession with classic cars into a thriving business which now has 800 Bongo-owning customers from all parts of Britain.

He stumbled across his first Bongo – almost literally – back in the days when he used to help his friends restore their cars.

Bongos were almost unknown in those days – certainly nowhere near the cult status they are approaching today – but Tim quickly spotted the potential of the one parked at his father's garage ('I thought it was a fantastic, clever, really versatile vehicle,' he says) and it was not long before he was using it for camping trips to Whitby.

'My friends thought it was a bit weird and said it wasn't very cool, but that didn't bother me,' he says. 'I just knew.'

It was not long before he started buying Bongos that had been written off by their owners as beyond repair, making them roadworthy again and selling them at a profit.

And he began to make a reputation as the Bongo man to go to . . .

'A few people started hearing my name, then a few more, and they began to ask me to look after theirs,' he says. 'And it just went from there. Word of mouth . . . Now people come here from all over the country.'

Not surprisingly, Tim no longer does all the work himself. To help him he has a team including his Dad David, a retired motor mechanic with 40 years' experience in the motor trade, his brother David Jr, an engineer, his friend and expert classic car restorer Andy, and ex detective Kev, who describes himself as 'a valeter and handyman'.

'We're always pretty busy,' he says, rather unnecessarily.

9

Irton

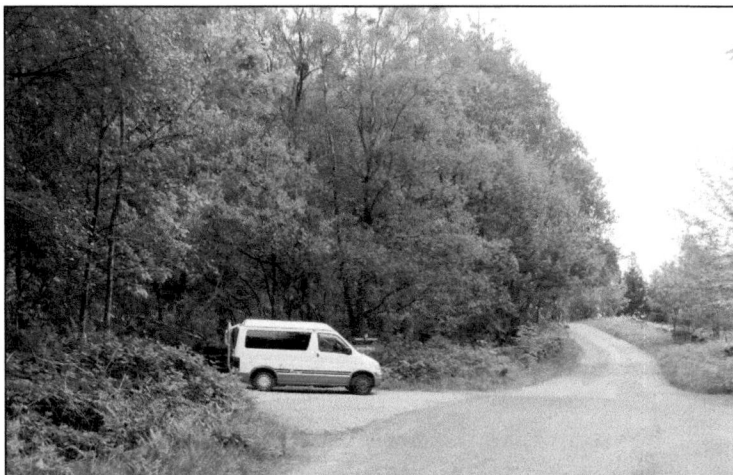

When it came to deciding upon somewhere to stop for my next Bongo Night I was not exactly spoiled for choice. Places whose names begin with I are hardly thick on the ground in Cumbria, and those that do – Ireby and Ivegill, for example – are not within the boundaries of the National Park.

So my search began and ended with a place which hardly seemed to exist as a place at all – Irton. True there is a small mountain called Irton Pike, a posh hotel called Irton Hall and a church called St Paul's Church, Irton, and when you get there you will find a signpost pointing somewhat optimistically to Irton, but no search of the Ordnance Survey map will ever produce a village or hamlet of that name.

Further investigation shows that Irton is part of a civil parish called Irton with Santon, and though there is indeed a small village called Santon there is no such individual place known as Irton.

Instead there is a hill – all 229 metres (751 feet) of it – which stands proud in the valley, giving splendid views across to the very much more dramatic outline of Scafell and Scafell Pike and, on a clear day, the sea beyond Seascale in the other direction, and it was to its lower slopes that I headed.

I found a small parking place, big enough for three or four cars, alongside one Forestry Commission sign proclaiming this to be Irton Pike and another urging visitors to stick to the waymarked paths so as not to spread disease among the vulnerable trees.

Which would have been fine if any waymarks had been visible.

Instead a well worn footpath disappeared into the forest from behind where I parked the Bongo, and then turned sharp left, hugging the contour as it wound around to the western side of the pike.

I took that path, seeing no sign of any other, and enjoyed an easy ramble through the wood, watching all the time for any opportunity to turn off it and climb what I guessed would be a steep route to the pike.

After more than a mile I realised I was leaving the hill behind and was in danger of striking out into the wilderness of Wasdale Common, which did not seem a good idea at that time of the evening, especially for a pensioner with no map, no emergency rations and no idea where on earth he was going.

For safety's sake I turned round to retrace my steps in the knowledge that the next day would give me more time to search for the ascent.

Just as I was getting back to where I had started I spotted a narrow, slightly trampled gap in the undergrowth on my left. Peering for a closer look I saw that just behind the bushes was an almost vertical scar where the mud had been disturbed between the rocks.

This, I reckoned, was as close as I was going to get to an official route to the summit.

The climb took me only about 20 minutes, though it was hard work for someone not used to such exertion, and when I emerged from between the conifers into a clearing at the top I saw the effort had been worthwhile – stupendous views in every direction, with the golden evening sunshine emphasising the dramatic character of the fells all around.

Almost immediately I saw a much more obvious path heading up to the pike from the north – from almost the opposite direction from which I had come.

That, then, was the way I was supposed to have come . . . and would be the way I would go back down the hill to the Bongo.

It was a rough but gentle zigzag walk through the trees, and it eventually turned into a wide track that snaked first north, then south around the lower slopes of the pike.

As I arrived at my parking place a sudden movement caught my eye among the trees alongside the Bongo.

A red squirrel was eyeing me from a thick branch, from which a couple of bird feeders were hanging.

Now there's nothing particularly unusual about red squirrels in the Lake District, but for me they have always been a reminder of how lucky I am to live in this part of the country.

In other places we might get excited by the sight even of a common grey squirrel, but here we look upon such animals as pests and try to trap and kill them because we know that their more beautiful cousins can't hope to survive against them.

Indeed, a few years ago red squirrels were common in my garden. At one time we could almost set our watches by them – for several weeks two of them would appear at about three o'clock every afternoon, taking nuts from the feeder among the trees on our lawn, then chasing each other on the grass, or swinging through the branches of the silver birch.

This one, at Irton Pike, was tamer than any others I had seen. It happily posed for my photographs, and watched with an interested eye as I walked up to the Bongo – almost within touching distance of it – and unlocked the door.

It took no notice as I climbed inside, did not flinch as I closed the noisy sliding door behind me and simply munched on a nut as I pressed my face to the glass for a better look through the window.

It played among the branches for many minutes, going through its full range of tricks – jumping and swinging just six feet in front of my eyes, as if out to impress me with its gymnastic skills.

I knew I could have found a meal just a couple of miles away, at the bridge which gives both the village of Santon Bridge and a pub its name, but I had enough food for the evening (an apple-topped pork pie, a packet of vegetable crisps and three different sorts of salad that I had bought on my drive down) so there was no need for me to go anywhere at all.

I was happy there in my parking place – undisturbed by anything other than an occasional passing car, the tapping of a distant woodpecker and the return, every few minutes, of my squirrel – and after a short walk through the forest on the other side of the road made up the bed and fell asleep.

I woke early the next morning. And when I lifted the blind beside my bed the squirrel was already busy outside, chomping nuts.

It had gone by the time a 4x4 pulled into the parking space on the other side of the road. An elderly woman dressed all in black climbed out and crossed the road towards me with two polythene tubs in her hands.

'Sorry to disturb your breakfast,' she said, smiling, as she noticed the big plateful of fried breakfast on the table in front of me. 'But the birds need theirs too.'

'You're not disturbing me at all,' I told her, grateful that she wasn't about to give me a telling-off for spending the night somewhere I shouldn't have. 'But if you were hoping to see the squirrel you're too late. He's been and gone.'

The woman told me this was an everyday occurrence. At about 8 o'clock every morning, seven days a week, all through the winter and spring, she would come here in her car to top up the bird feeders with seeds and nuts.

'It all started with just one robin,' she told me with an even bigger smile. 'That was about five years ago, but then the robin was joined by a few blue tits and some nuthatches, and then a few other species too . . . and just last year the squirrel started coming. We hadn't seen red squirrels here for years.'

Sharing a few minutes with a delightful old lady who derived so much pleasure from doing such simple things had provided a supremely uplifting start to my day, so I found myself asking her for suggestions of what to do next to make the best of the rest of it.

I had thought of walking across the fields to the church, I told her, but that was before I looked at the map and found that there were no fields and no obvious footpaths in that direction.

'You should go to a place nobody else knows about,' she said enigmatically as we spread my OS map across the Bongo's bonnet.

Her finger traced the route of a footpath through the trees opposite – a variation of the late walk I had done the night before.

It was a beautiful walk through the pine forest, she said, and if at the bottom of the hill I veered sharply to the left, along a path that was hardly worthy of the name, it would take me to Parkgate Tarn, a small and peaceful lake on which I would find ducks and butterflies and a welcome escape from any cares that might be troubling my busy world.

'It's a pity you're a bit too early for the water lilies,' she said.

And then with another smile: 'But, then, you can't have everything.'

She was right. It was a very beautiful lake, glistening like a blanket of jewels in the morning sunshine, and, though the ducks scattered at my first footfall, the butterflies stayed to play above the water lily buds. There was not a sound.

After a few minutes sitting on a log enjoying the tranquillity I began to wonder how I might spend the rest of my morning.

It was a beautiful day, perfect for walking, and I had not gone anywhere near far enough yet to even begin to feel tired, so I just had to go on.

A quick look at my map told me that, though there were no direct paths to it, if I continued on through the forest I would soon come to a wider track which would take me past a farm and then on to a road, which would lead me to another footpath over the fields to the church.

It took me only a little over half an hour.

St Paul's is a lovely little church, standing all alone in the middle of open countryside, with cows munching on the grass beside the fence that leads to the door.

It is known for its Anglo Saxon stone cross, that stands 10ft high in the churchyard, with intricate fret patterning and vine scrolls that are still almost perfect even after more than 1,000 years, and for the incredibly vivid windows – full of deep reds, greens and blues – designed by the master Victorian arts and crafts man Sir Edward

Burne-Jones, whose stained glass is also the highlight of St Martin's Church in Brampton, the small town about five miles from where I live.

But it was something else that interested me more.

Standing almost casually against the church wall was a plaque commemorating Captain Daniel Brocklebank, a local shipbuilder and master mariner who, I vaguely remembered, founded the business which went on to play a major part in the development of the Cunard shipping line.

It was Daniel who in the late 1700s founded the shipyard in Whitehaven, 15 miles up the coast, that became Brocklebanks – later run by his sons Thomas and John, and then by his grandsons, Ralph and Thomas Jr.

In the 19th century this family business was one of the world's major shipping lines, with 50 ships trading on routes to India, China and South America.

In the early 1900s it was bought, bit by bit, by Cunard, and though the Brocklebank name survived in that company's cargo division for many years, it faded and then closed altogether in the mid 1980s.

For someone who spent his childhood dreaming of joining the merchant navy, and who changed his mind only when as a teenager he realised that a life at sea would not be compatible with the happy family life he also craved, that old stone – and another Brocklebank memorial, to Thomas, a replica Anglo Saxon cross that looked very much like the genuine one just a few paces away – was even more fascinating than any wonderful stained glass or ancient relic.

Not for the first time I counted myself lucky that my Bongo Nights – my unplanned, spontaneous trips to some of Cumbria's lesser known corners – had a habit of turning into something much more interesting than I had ever expected.

10

Junction 38

Never did I think that one day I'd spend the night sleeping under a bridge. Not like some poor homeless old chap with a scrawny dog on the end of a piece of string, sleeping in a tattered eiderdown and cardboard box under a bridge in London, it's true.

But as I made my bed in the Bongo, parked almost under a motorway, the similarities were enough to bring a wry smile to my face.

A bridge under the M6 would not normally be my choice for a comfortable Bongo Night, but sometimes a man's left with no choice . . .

I was up to J in my A-Z tour of the Lake District, and the fact is that there was nowhere else to go that began with J.

I had managed to find a village called Johnby, but that, while in the county of Cumbria, was not within the National Park, which was one of the criteria I had set myself when I had embarked on this adventure.

I had found mention of Jack's Rake, but discounted that on many grounds – not least the fact that it's part of a dangerous and often deadly scramble up a mountain in Great Langdale.

And I had spotted Jack's Plantation, a small wood in the middle of Grizedale Forest, which was miles away from the nearest potential parking spot.

But apart from that ... nothing.

It was Tricia who came to my aid . . . when in a blinding flash the solution came to her.

'How about Junction 38?'

'Brilliant!' I said – and I called her a genius.

Junction 38 on the M6 is not itself within the National Park, not by a few yards.

The park's eastern boundary runs alongside the motorway for a few miles, virtually hugging the hard shoulder of the northbound carriageway as it approaches the turning to the village of Tebay, so it is possible to see the motorway – and, more importantly from my point of view, the junction – from several places which are technically still inside the Lake District.

So any of those locations would suit me well enough.

The spot I settled on exceeded all my expectations – down a decently tarmacked lane that led through a bridge under the motorway until it petered out, first into a muddy track and then into a footpath which wound its way up to Tebay on the other side.

Just before the lane went under the bridge – and therefore only just before it left the National Park – there was a nice level grassy area, big enough for the Bongo but not much more.

I must have been just inches inside the Lake District.

On one side – away from the motorway – was an undulating field full of uninquisitive sheep, while ahead of me was the pretty little village of Roundthwaite, with the land rising steeply beyond it to the higher ground of Grayrigg Forest and the beginnings of the Lakeland mountains.

It was as perfect a spot as I could reasonably have hoped for.

But it was early in the afternoon and I had some exploring to do yet (I was, after all, in a part of the world I had never stopped in before, and I wanted to taste just a little of what it had to offer).

Like Borrowdale, for example.

I was very familiar with Borrowdale – it's a beautiful valley just south of Keswick and a place where I have walked, camped and paddled my kayak many times in the past.

But this was another Borrowdale, another beautiful valley, but a different one, which has little in common – least of all the thousands of tourists – with the much better known cousin whose name it shares.

I drove a mile or so south from my Bongo spot, took a quick turn right into the valley and parked beside a handful of other cars just before a farm gate blocked the way.

I had no intention of tackling one of the big walks of that area – proper fellwalkers, I knew, would at that moment be tackling the route along the ridge I could see above me – but instead was set on the track ahead of me, that led deep into the valley and (if I got that far, which I knew was unlikely) eventually on to the A6 north-south main road a few miles north of Kendal.

It was an easy, beautiful – if muddy – walk, winding gently up the valley, far away from civilisation or any other person and with just the cheerful gurgling of the Borrow Beck for company.

And then I met a little white dog.

Now, as I have said before, I don't share other people's enthusiasm for dogs.

I hate the way they yap at me, jump up at me and – while their owners tell me 'he's only being friendly' – try to mate with my left leg.

But this one, I have to admit, was rather sweet.

He was a Highland terrier and he scampered up to me and, with what (if I were of a more schmaltzy frame of mind) I would describe as a smile on his face, sat down beside me.

Around the bend ahead of me then came his owner, an old lady who (with her big smile, rosy cheeks and white hair tied up in a tight bun) would, if we'd given her a floury apron, have been the friendly cook in some children's storybook.

'He likes you,' she said.

And to prove it he jumped up and wiped his muddy paws down my jeans.

There is something about some dogs – and their owners – that I'm willing to forgive.

And this pair, the old lady and her cute little dog, had it.

'How do you keep him so clean?' I asked, eyeing the dog's astonishingly clean white coat, spoiled only by a thick splash of mud on his feet.

'I don't do anything,' she told me.

'You must bath him after a walk like this, surely?'

'Never!' she said. 'That's the best way. I just let nature take its course.'

And then, giggling, she added: 'I think I've just persuaded myself never to have another bath either. I'll just let nature take its course with me from now on too!'

She walked on, chuckling, and as I continued up the track I counted myself lucky that the only person I had met was such a cheery soul.

And then I heard the sound of a vehicle coming up behind me.

A minibus.

Followed by a car.

Followed by a white van.

And a little way behind, a teenaged girl on a bike.

I stood aside to let the convoy past, puzzled that such an out-of-the-way place should attract quite such a gathering.

Half a mile further on I saw why.

A campsite had been put up – several tents, campervans, portaloos, a big gazebo and strings of flags – beside my track, on just about the only flat piece of ground in the valley

So much for my tranquil piece of heaven!

I stopped, sat on a rock for a few minutes (facing the other way, so I could pretend that the campsite behind me was not there) and then walked back the way I had come.

I met three more cars as I went, and when I spotted an open window in one I asked the driver what was going on.

'It's a private family party,' he told me – carefully emphasising the word 'private', I thought, to tell me that I would not be welcome to join them even if I wanted to.

My original plan had been to park the Bongo at my overnight spot, then walk along the track and the footpath into Tebay for supper at the

Cross Keys, the village's only pub, but I had to think again when I found the way was blocked by the sort of puddle which would have made it impassable even with the wellies that I did not have.

Instead I drove the three miles into the village, parking right outside the pub's front door.

Tebay is a village whose best days, I think it's fair to say, have gone.

It's a long, straggling place that seems to be only just hanging on – both literally, since the landscape falls dramatically down towards the River Lune, and figuratively thanks to the decline it has entered since the important railway connections upon which its prosperity depended closed in the 1960s.

Tebay had always been a remote, hill farming village, but the coming of the railways – Lancaster & Carlisle Railway and the cross-Pennine South Durham & Lancashire Union Railway met there – gave it a whole new and unplanned-for lease of life,

Both railways had locomotive depots there, which led to not just a smart little station and a cattle market being built to cope with the demand, but also an influx of railway workers and five rows of houses built especially for them.

Even the parish church – an impressive building, built on a slope and with a little bell tower that has a conical roof so that it looks like a Scottish castle – owed its existence to the railways, being built with contributions from some of the directors of the railway companies.

Since it was evening, it was locked when I got there, which was a pity because I would like to have seen the interior, which was built with two-tone bricks like many of the stations of the time.

Sadly for Tebay, the railways, having built the place up, could do little to help prevent it falling back down again.

Business steadily declined from the early 1950s until it was lost altogether following the Beeching report of 1965.

The old station buildings and platforms were demolished in the early 1970s and today there is no sign of them, although some of the sidings still remain, for use by engineering trains.

Indeed the village's connection with the railways is cemented these days by memories of a disaster in February 2004 when four rail workers died after they were hit by a wagon loaded with 16 tonnes of steel which ran away from a maintenance yard near Shap, five kilometres north.

The wagon had faulty brakes and was being held just by wooden chocks in front of its wheels, and when these were dislodged during the unloading of part of its load, the wagon began to move down the hill towards Tebay.

In pitch darkness and near silence it reached speeds of up to 40mph until, without warning, it struck and killed the four men, injuring five others, who were working on the line just north of the village.

Two men were later jailed for manslaughter, one for nine years and one for two.

The Cross Keys is a huge pub. That anyway was my first impression as I walked in through the door in search of my supper.

The bar was on the far side of a substantially sized dining area, and beyond that was an enormous restaurant – nicely laid, with tablecloths and shining cutlery, but no customers – and through the door past that was a very spacious beer garden which boasted fantastic views of the M6 and, if you lifted your eyes a bit, of the Lake District fells in the distance.

I confess I prefer somewhere a bit smaller, a bit more intimate – a place where customers have to rub shoulders, and therefore talk to each other whether they like it or not (a bit more like the Newfield Inn at Seathwaite-in-Dunnerdale, for example).

Which is not to say it wasn't welcoming. The staff, and the handful of customers gathered at the bar, were friendly enough but . . .

Well, maybe I just wasn't in the mood.

I drove back to my place under the bridge and, following my usual routine, played my guitar for a while, listened to the radio . . . and slept soundly.

Any fears I had of being disturbed by the noise of the traffic were ill founded. Being below the motorway, rather than level with it or above it, the sound seemed to pass over my head, so though I was vaguely conscious of traffic whizzing past just a few yards away, the noise it made amounted to little more than a lullaby.

There was nothing to be decided next morning – apart from where to have breakfast.

Tebay is famous both for the motorway service stations which bear its name and for the nearby Junction 38 truckstop, all of which are run by Westmorland Limited, a company founded by a local hill farming family after the M6 was built, cutting through their land.

John Dunning and his wife Barbara viewed the M6 not as the death of their farm, but as the beginning of a whole new chapter in how they ran it.

The first Tebay Services were opened – as a small 30 seat café serving home cooked, locally sourced food – in 1972 and nearly half a century on, that small café has developed into a major business, still owned by the family, and now encompassing motorway service stations not just in Cumbria but in Scotland and Gloucestershire too.

And, since 1986, it has also run the Junction 38 Truckstop, reckoned by many to be the finest transport café in Britain.

To say that the Tebay Services are unlike any other is not doing them justice.

They have no burger bars, sandwich franchises or mini versions of high street supermarkets.

Instead they each have a farmshop, selling meat and vegetables as good as any you could find anywhere, and a restaurant where you can buy a home-made meal that's a pleasure to eat.

Their service stations are supposed to be for the benefit of travellers, and the idea that they might become destinations in their own right is, I gather, frowned upon by the authorities, but I know for a fact (because I have done it myself) they are so good that locals will happily go there too, to do their shopping or have a good meal.

Faced by a choice between an award-winning Motorway Services which I had visited many times before and an award-winning truckstop which I hadn't . . . I chose the truckstop.

I had little idea what to expect, apart from a vague understanding that truckstops these days were a far cry from the grubby and tacky transport cafes of my youth.

Even so, I was not expecting what I found at Junction 38 – a restaurant, bar, shops (of both the corner and farm variety), easy chairs, clean toilets, showers.

Everything, in other words, that you might expect from a good Motorway Services, but without the noise, bustle and queues.

I ordered myself a 'light breakfast' – sausage, bacon, fried egg, hash brown, mushrooms and black pudding, with two slices of toast – having decided against the heavier version (add baked beans, tomato, fried bread and haggis to make it a ten-item plateful).

And afterwards, realising that a walk would probably undo a little of the harm done by my feast, I drove a mile up the road to the last port of call of my trip – Castle Howe, the remains of a medieval motte and bailey castle which, though it sits right beside it, I had never noticed on any of my hundreds of journeys up and down the M6.

It was a muddy walk to get there, but rewarded by that feeling you get when you've found somewhere you know you really should have found many years before.

Castle Howe is a splendid place in its modest and mysterious way.

It was a fortification built near the intersection between the River Lune and Birk Beck – presumably to control trade along the river from the fertile agricultural areas downstream – and though it has been badly eroded by past floods the nine foot high motte is still visible above the bailey and even an inexpert eye like mine could make out the vague traces of a rampart and ditch on one side.

Not a place to attract the Lake District tourists in their thousands, perhaps, but enough to remind me again that my nights in the Bongo had a habit of throwing up interesting places where I least expected them.

11
Kettlewell

Kettlewell is probably the Lake District place that has played a bigger part in my life than any other. Which is a strange thing to say about a car park.

If you look on the internet you will find many satisfied customers extolling its virtues, for everything from its 'glorious views', its 'great' picnic spots, its 'perfect' beach for launching canoes and even its 'ideal' location for going for a swim.

Its only drawback in the eyes of the average tourist, it seems, is that it has neither cafe nor toilet . . . which some of us might be tempted to describe as something of a plus.

Although I've always drawn the line at swimming in something as obviously chilly as a Cumbrian lake, I have had many happy times there so it seemed appropriate to include it here when I reached K in my A-Z of the Lake District.

Kettlewell, according to my guidebook-writing friend Mark Richards, gets its name from being a 'perceived boiling pool on the lake' – the lake, in this case, being Derwentwater, that magnificent stretch of water that reaches from the bustling excitement of Keswick in the north to the quiet foothills of Castle Crag in the south.

Kettlewell is about half way down it – a National Trust car park nestling so close to the water it is almost possible to sit with your front wheels in the water.

'There's a small pebble beach and glorious views out over the lake and fells,' says one enthusiast. 'It makes a nice little stop off for lunch if you're in the Borrowdale area. It's also perfect for launching a kayak, or going for a paddle or even a swim.'

Launching a kayak is exactly what I know Kettlewell best for.

Ever since we each bought our kayaks, Kettlewell is the place from which Tricia and I have most often launched them.

From there it is an easy paddle north, zigzagging between the islands, to Keswick, with its promise of ice creams or, in the winter, hot Cornish pasties to keep any tired limbs moving.

But if you head south, instead of north, a delightful route takes you across the head of the lake and into the mouth of the River Derwent, from where a gentle paddle against the current takes you towards the pretty little village of Grange, Castle Crag and, in the distance, the Jaws of Borrowdale.

Whether you're actually going to get to Grange is always in doubt, because too much rain – or too little – can make the river unnavigable.

On one occasion, it's true, at the time when heartbreaking floods were hitting other parts of Cumbria with much less welcome results, the water was so high we had the excitement of being able to paddle our kayaks across what were normally fields, so opening up vistas not usually visible to us.

But more often heavy rain in the preceding hours can make it impossible to make headway up the river. Even in the summer, when the water level can be hoped to be at its lowest and most tranquil, a sudden heavy shower can make it flow too fast for a pensioner in a canoe, and if it doesn't rain at all the water level can drop so far that the only solution is to get out and walk.

When it is possible to paddle all – or nearly all – the way to Grange it is a wonderful, leisurely trip, maybe punctuated by a picnic along the way, or an ice cream when you get there, on which you are almost guaranteed to see breeding barnacle geese and, if you're lucky, kingfishers.

Although it's an almost perfect family playground, Kettlewell has one major drawback – it can also be a danger zone.

Too often we have seen small children splashing around at the edge of the lake, under the inattentive eyes of their parents who mistakenly believe that such a piece of paradise could not hold any danger to their offspring.

Yet the lakes of the Lake District are dangerous – just as dangerous as the mountains, maybe – and should always be approached with caution.

And it's not just the danger of children drowning under the summer sun.

It is not many years since the police had to send out warnings to people tempted to enjoy the frozen lake . . . by walking on it – some more than 50 yards from the shore – not knowing how much, or how little, ice was beneath their feet.

There have never, as far as I know, been any warnings of the danger posed at Kettlewell to old men in campervans.

But maybe there should have been.

For it was there that I nearly broke my back.

I was there in my Bongo because a campervan-owning friend told me that the chap trying to sell National Trust memberships there told her that although overnight parking was not officially allowed the Trust turned a blind eye to it if the vehicles had membership badges on their windscreens.

I have noticed that the National Trust has, since then, put up prominent signs banning camping and parking overnight, but back then my conscience was clear and as a long standing member of the National Trust I needed no further invitation. So I headed for Kettlewell, arriving late in the afternoon, determined – despite the intermittent rain – to set off from there to walk around the lake, stopping off two-thirds of the way round in the Dog and Gun pub in Keswick, an establishment where the range and quality of the local beers on offer is matched only by their superb goulash (large or small, meaty or vegetarian, with dumplings).

As I have said before, I'm not a particularly enthusiastic fell-walker – the fact that I've done nearly half the 214 Wainwrights (the Cumbrian fells Alfred Wainwright listed as being worth climbing) owes more to happenstance than any wish to get them all ticked off as many people do, but a ten-mile walk around a lovely lake on a summer's afternoon is something to be savoured. Especially when it includes a visit to one of my favourite pubs.

I walked fast, as I always do, and my spirits were not dampened even by the frequent showers which saw me putting on and taking off my cagoule so often that in the end I thought 'Oh sod it!' and simply left it off and got wet.

By the time I walked into the Dog and Gun I was soaked to the skin and quite literally steaming. My hair was plastered to my head. My trousers, soaked from mid-thigh to ankle, were clinging to my legs, and my walking boots squelched whenever I moved my feet on the flagstone floor.

The pub was heaving with customers and as I approached the bar the landlord was busy turning away a family of four, telling them they had no hope of getting a table within the foreseeable future so they might be best advised to go somewhere else.

I had no intention of going anywhere else (my heart was set on a goulash, for one thing) so I gave the landlord a damp grin and told him I'd have a pint and would then be happy to wait for as long as it took to find somewhere to sit.

In most pubs the bar staff would simply have told me that though I was welcome to stand by the bar until a table became available I'd have to find that table myself, but here the landlord was going out of his way – literally – to make me welcome. He told me there might be no need to wait and, in what I considered a superb example of customer service, he came out from behind the bar and went around his pub looking for a table which had space for just one bedraggled walker.

He established me on a table occupied by a middle-aged couple who welcomed me with sympathetic smiles and told me they would not mind at all if I tucked into my pint and my goulash (large) in front of them while they were genteely sipping their lemonade and limes.

The goulash was as delicious as I knew it would be, and I scoffed it, probably far too quickly, while finding out as much as I could about my two table-mates. She was a Yorkshire lass, she told me (unnecessarily, since her accent betrayed as much), but she now lived in Alsace, where not long before she had married a Frenchman, on whose behalf she apologised for the fact that he could not join in our conversation since he could neither speak nor understand a word of English.

They waited until I'd finished my goulash, then excused themselves because they had to go back to their guesthouse for a supper that they admitted would probably not be as good as my goulash.

With a table to myself I was now in something of a predicament. I wanted – no, I needed – another pint, but I knew that, with the pub still full of people looking around desperately for somewhere to sit. if I went to the bar I would be in danger of losing my seat.

I caught the eye of one of the crowd in front of me, a young man leaning on the bar, who, like his girlfriend, was making short work of a pint of local Landlord ale. He leaned forward to hear what I was obviously about to say to him.

'You're very welcome to sit here at this table,' I told him. 'As long as you don't mind me coming back and sharing it with you when I've got another pint.'

It never entered my head that, though they were obviously foreign, they might not understand what I was saying.

And the speed at which they left their places at the bar and joined me at my table told me they understood very well . . . and did not mind at all.

I'm pretty quick at deciding if I like people (too quick, probably, because I often find myself disliking people on first impressions, only to have to revise my opinion later on when I've got to know them better). And these two I liked immediately.

I soon discovered that his name was Pascal and hers was Julia, and that they were one half of a folk-rock band called Postcards from Beirut, who – though the other two members had gone straight home after playing at a music festival in Oxford – had chosen to take the scenic route back to Lebanon and ended up in Cumbria.

'It's because we're a couple,' Julia told me, as if that explained everything.

Pascal told me he had a love of English beer – something he demonstrated by the speed at which he drank it – and that they had spent part of the day on a tour of Keswick brewery (an establishment that I, a near-local, did not even know existed).

And Julia told me how much they loved the Lake District, despite the rain, and how lucky they were to have ended up by chance in Keswick on their circuitous journey home to the Middle East.

I stayed with Pascal and Julia in the pub until the time came when I knew I would have to leave if I was to get back to Kettlewell and the Bongo before it got dark. As I left Pascal called after me 'If you're ever passing Beirut please call in and see us'.

As I walked back along the shore of Derwentwater – a beautiful walk even in the half light – I told myself that my Bongo Nights were going rather well. And meeting some very lovely people was turning out to be a bonus I had not expected.

(I have kept in touch with Pascal and Julia ever since, and was alarmed to hear that they only narrowly escaped when their home in the heart of Beirut was wrecked when a store full of ammonium nitrate exploded, killing more than 200 people, in August 2020. Julia, who happened to be behind a pillar when the blast occurred, was unhurt, but Pascal's face and left side were shredded by flying glass and he needed complicated surgery to repair the damage done to his leg.)

Back at the Kettlewell car park I found that I had it to myself . . . apart from a big old fashioned campervan which, closer inspection showed, was in fact just a works van which had two canoes on the top and not much more than a couple of mattresses and a camping cooker inside. It was home to a couple from Lancashire and their nine-year-old son.

Over the camp fire that they had built on the beach to keep the midges away, they told me they had been there for three days, and that the National Trust warden was well aware of it and had not voiced one word of complaint.

I moved the Bongo closer to the lake so I'd be able to look out of the window and see the view when I woke up, and settled down to a night's sleep that I knew would be a good one. No doggers. No boy racers. No wondering if some jobsworth would wake me up in the night to tell me I should not be there. Just the sound of the water lapping gently over the pebbles in the wind.

I was brought heavily back down to earth – almost literally – the next morning. I was tidying up the Bongo after breakfast when I stood up in the back and leaned over the front seats to raise the electric blinds with the switches on the dashboard.

Then, without looking or even thinking, I went to sit down on the bed which I knew was behind me. Except it wasn't. I had forgotten that I had already stowed the bed away. So instead of sitting on the soft mattress, made even softer by a thick duvet, I fell to the floor, smashing my back against the unforgiving metal and wood frame of the bed. It was like having a 16-stone hammer blow to my back.

I sat on the floor for several minutes, folded up in a Z-shape between the front seats and the stashed-away bed, gasping for breath and totally unable to move. I knew the only people likely to hear me if I called for help were the couple and their young son in the van at the other end of the car park, and there was no sign that they were awake yet.

I reckoned that I had two choices – stay where I was until the day trippers began to arrive, in the hope that one of them might come close enough to hear my cries, or somehow extricate myself . . . no matter how painful it might be. I chose the latter. I slowly rolled onto my side and, after grabbing the top of the cupboards alongside me, dragged myself to my knees.

I was still on my knees when I got out of the van, and still doubled up as I slowly stumbled around the outside of it and, gasping from the pain, slumped into the driver's seat.

I needed to warn Tricia, but didn't want to alarm her, so sent her a text: 'On my way. Could do with hot bath cos I've bashed my back. I'm OK but will have a bruise! See you soon.'

That afternoon my doctor told me to lift my shirt. 'Christ! That's going to bloody hurt!' he said (stating the obvious, I thought). He established that I had probably not done myself any lasting damage. I had somehow managed to twist my body immediately before the impact, so the blow had caught me slightly to the side, in the space between my hip bone and my ribs, rather than directly across my spine, so with luck I had suffered nothing worse than a very painful soft tissue injury.

He prescribed me codeine for the pain, told me to go back to him if I noticed I was peeing blood (that would have been a sign of a damaged kidney) . . . and wished me luck in any further adventures I might have in what he called my 'killer campervan'.

12
Langdale

There are all kinds of reasons why Bongo Nights don't go according to plan, and most of them do not involve almost causing myself a life-changing injury.

Some are not as comfortable as I had hoped, not as quiet and not in such beautiful surroundings, and some just go off in tangents that I could not have foreseen.

My night in the Langdales was a perfect example.

Who would have guessed that what was turning into a disappointing night there would be saved by my meeting a woman who, just two years before, had been a man?

I had chosen that location for just one reason – its pub.

The Old Dungeon Ghyll Hotel describes itself as 'a unique Lake District hotel' located in a 'remote and unspoiled valley', which has been offering 'accommodation and sustenance for 300 years or more'.

Anyone wanting a 'cosy getaway far away from the stresses of modern day life' need look no further, its website says.

Even allowing for the ad man's hyperbole it sounded my sort of place.

And when I heard that the owners allowed campervans to stay in its car park overnight – and that once a week it hosted a music night in its bar, I knew I had to give it a try.

I confess I had imagined that there, in such an isolated place on an almost out-of-season Wednesday night, I would probably have the car park to myself . . . and find that the 'music night' would consist of the bored-looking landlord playing his accordion in a corner of his deserted bar, smiling a relieved welcome at me as I walked in to double his clientele for the evening.

So much for expectations!

By the time I arrived the pub's own car park was full – yes, of campervans mostly, parked so tightly next to each other that the occupants of one would later surely be kept awake by the noise of the occupants of the next one turning over in bed – but happily there is a big National Trust car park immediately alongside the pub's own, so I pulled in there, parked with the bonnet cosily against a chest-high dry stone wall, and set off towards the rousing chorus that, even with the Bongo windows firmly closed, I could hear drifting from the bar.

The pub was packed with people, many of them standing up and boasting of how many fells they had conquered that day, and of how many thousand feet they had climbed in how few minutes. Some were gathered at the tables, eating what looked like hearty meals, and doing their best to ignore the efforts of the four old men playing (two guitars, a banjo and a fiddle) in the corner.

'When's this fucking band going stop?' one man wearing the inevitable uniform of the committed fell walker (a blue sweatshirt boldly emblazoned with ACTIVE! in yellow letters, a green gilet, and khaki trousers with black reinforcements on the knees) asked his friend as I squeezed past.

'Not until they've got us soddin' dancing,' his friend said bitterly.

I pushed my way to the bar (such people don't bother to make room for newcomers, I find), ordered a pint of something named after one of the better known local mountains, and looked around for somewhere to sit.

I nodded hopefully at an empty chair

'OK if I perch here?' I asked of a man wearing a T-shirt stamped with 'Fellwalkers do it in muddy boots' in bright red letters.

'It's taken,' he muttered, though he did not say – and I could not see – by whom.

I looked again and decided to take a chance with a friendlier-looking middle aged couple sitting at the only other table that was not fully occupied.

'Of course,' they said in unison, both smiling and throwing me gestures of welcome.

These were Helen and David, from Norfolk, who had come to the Lake District, and were enjoying it, they said, despite the fact that a ruptured hamstring – suffered just a week before they had come – meant he was barely able to walk across the bar, let alone climb a mountain.

'We were looking forward to a good week's walking, but . . . ,' he said, lifting his eyebrows in an expression of calm acceptance. 'Still, it's lovely though, isn't it?'

I had barely made a dent in my pint before they got up to leave, assuring me it was nothing personal, but they had a campervan in the campsite just down the road and they needed to get back to it before it started raining again.

I was now alone in a pub which, though not actually unfriendly, was not exactly friendly either.

It seemed full of people who wanted to boast about their mountaineering exploits, and were becoming increasingly exasperated because they could not make their voices heard above the music men in the corner.

And the music men in the corner, though competent in their craft, seemed to have no interest in engaging anyone else with it.

It was, I thought, going to be a long night . . .

And then Diane came in.

She had a briefcase under her arm, a pile of posters in one hand and a roll of sticky tape in the other.

She fixed a poster to every available surface – on both sides of the door, on the wall by the window, on the wall behind the bar and on the wall next to where the old men were singing, and one of them was close enough for me to read without budging from my seat:

Diane's Autobiography.
Living in the wrong body.
An inspiring story about being born as a boy
but now transcending into a woman
On sale here today £5
Please see Diane for payment.
Money raised goes to her medical expenses

I looked (I hope I didn't stare) at her and concluded that, yes, at a push, this petite, well turned-out person with the very shapely ankles might once have been taken for a man.

Thanks to the posters she had so helpfully put up in front of me, I already knew the outline of her story . . . and I was pretty well able to guess some of the rest.

She made her way around the bar, laughing and chatting with people who were total strangers to her and I confess I couldn't take my eyes off her.

What pain, what fear, what challenges she must have gone through.

What guts to have faced a life such as she had had . . . and still come up smiling.

What courage to walk into a remote Cumbrian pub (and Cumbrian pubs are not always known for the broadmindedness of their customers) as a woman who had once been a man.

And what even greater courage to advertise the fact and be willing to talk about it!

She sat down at a table and talked for many minutes to the couple she met there, then moved to the next table, and the next . . . she moved around almost every table in the place but for some reason never came to mine.

I realised that if I was to rescue my evening I had to take the initiative.

So I got up and walked to her.

'I'm guessing you're Diane – would you like to join me at my table?'

It was, I was aware, the first time in my life I had used such an unvarnished chat-up line to a woman in a pub.

I talked to Diane for more than an hour and it was the most extraordinary conversation I have ever had.

To have gone through all that she had gone through, all the years of pain and confusion and never knowing how people were going to react to her, and to come out still smiling and at ease with the world, was a remarkable, humbling thing.

'You're so brave,' I told her more than once.

'I don't think I am,' she said. 'I just did what I had to do.'

'That was brave.'

'Oh . . . thank you.'

I knew that I would never get a better opportunity to talk to someone like her, to open a window into a world that – thankfully – I would have no other chance of entering.

But equally I did not want to disgrace myself by causing her hurt or offence.

'My wife sometimes says I jump in with both feet, saying things or asking things that I shouldn't say or ask,' I told her. 'It's the journalist in me. But if I ask you anything you don't like, or would rather not answer, I apologise in advance. Just tell me to go to hell.'

'Don't worry,' she said, smiling. 'There's nothing left that hasn't already been asked by someone sometime. I'm past getting upset and past being hurt.'

And so she told me her story.

Diane (she was in Langdale because she too had a campervan) was born in Chesterfield in April 1959, and in those days her name was Damien and her father was so excited to have a son to go with his two daughters he went straight out and bought a train set.

By the time she was five she realised she did not feel right being a boy and with her sisters' encouragement started dressing up in their clothes.

When she was 14 her father caught her wearing her sister's silk pyjamas and she 'confessed' and told her parents she did not want to be a boy any more.

By then other children were intimidating her because she was 'different' – they had noticed she preferred netball and rounders to football and cricket, and needlework and cooking to metalwork and woodwork.

And bullying became a regular feature of her life.

To escape it, as she got older, she bought a motorbike, grew a beard, let her hair grow long and developed a liking for the music of such people as Black Sabbath, Meatloaf and Led Zeppelin.

'I thought nobody would bully me any more if I looked like a rough, tough son of a bitch,' she told me. 'And I was right. It worked. But I still wasn't happy.

'What they didn't know was that underneath that hard and rough exterior was a kind and soft person who was wearing stockings and suspenders and frilly lace knickers beneath his bike gear.'

Through it all she worked as a man in heavy industry and had a succession of girlfriends – Diane was keen to tell me that though she did not feel male, she felt, and still feels, an ordinary male's attraction to 'ladies' – and married one of them.

She fathered a much loved daughter, suffered a divorce, went through the pleasure and pain of love affairs, maintained a successful career as an engineer . . . and whenever she got the chance changed into the clothes of the woman she longed to be.

She was 57 before she made the decision, at last, to become a woman, starting on a process which involved doctors, psychologists, psychiatrists and numerous appointments at a gender identity clinic, and a year later took one of the most difficult steps of all – telling the men she worked with.

Nearly all of them said she had their full support, and many told her she was not telling them anything they had not already worked out for themselves.

When I met her Diane had changed her name by deed poll, begun a course of hormone treatment to make her skin softer, her hair silkier and her breasts bigger and was longing for the day when she could afford a surgeon to remove what she describes as her 'unwanted bits'.

There were many aspects to my conversation with Diane that I found surprising.

First was the feeling – no, the knowledge – that I was talking to a woman.

Second was that I was talking to an extraordinarily courageous one.

Third was the fact that I liked her and admired her and felt just as comfortable in her company as I would in that of any woman I got on with.

I often think of her still, and I hope she is happy.

13
Martindale

One of the advantages of living in Cumbria (apart from the quality of life and sheer beauty of the countryside, of course) is that I've had time to get to know some of the Lake District's lesser known places.

Keswick, Ambleside and Bowness-on-Windermere are all very well – and many times I have enjoyed the bustle and busyness to be found there – but usually, given the choice, I will opt for somewhere away from the commercialism and the camera toting crowds of tourists.

Ask any 'local' (and I count myself as local even though I live 15 miles outside the boundary of the National Park) and they will have a favourite place where, despite the hordes just down the road, they can find peace and solitude.

One of my such places is Martindale – a magical valley tucked away on the 'wrong' side of Ullswater, at the end of a five-mile no-through-road, where great fells like the Nab and Beda Fell look down upon lowlands which are usually deserted apart from a handful of sheep and cows – or, at the right time of year, deer.

Indeed, if Martindale is known at all, it is for the red deer stags that come down from the fells in October to begin their annual rut.

The sight of majestic great beasts displaying themselves to their female admirers is a very special thing, and the sound of their roaring (the encircling fells turn the valley into a huge natural amphitheatre around which it echoes and reverberates) can surely be guaranteed to send a tingle down the spine of even the most hard hearted of humans.

It is no surprise that Martindale has become something of a tourist attraction at this time of year – albeit only to those lucky enough to be in the know.

So it is not unusual to find as many as, ooh maybe half a dozen people, getting up early to be there just after sunrise, when the spectacle is at its most awe inspiring.

For a man with a campervan it helps that there is a spot – just a couple of miles from where the road ends and visitors have to get out and walk to the best viewpoints – which ranks as one of the best wildcamping places in the whole of the Lake District.

Four miles south from the busy village of Pooley Bridge, past all the campsites, past the posh people's favourite hotel, the Sharrow Bay, and past the little pier where the Ullswater Steamers deposit any passengers adventurous enough to tackle the beautiful but quite strenuous 6½ mile walk back to Glenridding, the road rises sharply via a series of hairpin bends until it levels out for a while before descending not quite as steeply into the Martindale valley.

And there at the top, opposite the beautiful little church of St Peter (known as the Martindale New Church, to differentiate it from the even lovelier 'Old Church' of St Martin half a mile further on) is a parking space – level, if prone to puddles – which makes an ideal overnight spot for anyone wanting to make an early start next morning to see the deer.

It was dark when I got there – or as dark as it was going to get under a bright full moon – but I got out of the Bongo and walked a little way along the road to the spot from where I could look down upon the glistening shape of Ullswater under the black silhouettes of Hallin Fell and Bonscale Pike.

There was not a sound to be heard apart from the breeze whistling through the trees as it flexed its muscles for the near gale that would hit us overnight.

It was too cold to spend long looking at the view, and even for me too early to go to bed, so the long evening gave me an opportunity to enjoy one of the few luxuries I have allowed myself for my Bongo Nights.

I had bought a small portable DVD player some years before, but had never made proper use of it because the only DVDs I had were full-length movies – and the Bongo is no place to watch a film if you want to stay awake to see how it finishes.

I had lost count of the times that, sitting wrapped in blankets in the Bongo in the dark, I had fallen asleep soon after the opening titles.

But this time I had something I thought I could manage – a boxed set I had bought earlier that day in a Carlisle charity shop of every one of the 42 one-hour episodes of 'Rumpole of the Bailey', my favourite ever TV series.

Sitting in my beloved Bongo, in one of my favourite places on earth, watching my favourite TV programme was a pretty good way to spend an evening . . . and I stayed awake (for just one episode) to enjoy it.

The night was a wild one, with the wind whistling through the trees and around the Bongo, and only occasionally dropping long enough for me to hear the owls calling from the conifers that surround the little church.

I slept fitfully, but was wide awake by 6.30, just as daylight was beginning to peer through the clouds.

By 7 o'clock (after cooking myself a 'Mexican' breakfast – a tortilla stuffed with cheese and ham, named in honour of all the relatives my nephew Richard brought into our family when he moved to Mexico and married a Mexican girl) I had driven the two miles to the end of the road and parked near the farm through which the footpath into the valley passes.

I was dismayed to find that another car was already parked there.

In the past I had always been the first – and sometimes the only – person in the valley, and I did not like the idea of having to share my piece of heaven with anybody else.

I met them after walking for just ten minutes – a middle aged couple, with their teenaged son and his girlfriend, all standing beside the path gazing through binoculars at a stag on the fellside.

They were so excited – and, like me, so full of wonderment – that I could not begrudge them their intrusion.

All around us stags were roaring, the echoes bouncing off the mountains to create a rhythm that, were I a dancer, I could probably have danced to.

And that is where I stood for half an hour. Just looking, just listening and just rejoicing in one of the greatest spectacles natural Britain has to offer.

Eventually I moved, but only so I could stand and watch and listen in a place just a little further into the valley.

In front of me grazed a herd of a dozen or so deer with a stag picked out in the early morning sunshine, trying his best to impress every one of them; behind me a single doe, standing proud on the skyline; to my left and to my right, more males, more females and more of that wonderful sound.

I had had my fill and was back at the Bongo by 11 o'clock, which allowed me plenty of time to make two more visits before going home for lunch.

The tiny church of St Martin's – the Old Church – lies at the start of Martindale valley and is almost lost among the trees there. Indeed, I passed it many times over the years before realising there was a church there at all.

The church, which is never locked although it is now used only once a month or so, is thought to have been built at the end of the 16th century, replacing a chapel which had been there in the 1200s.

One of the trees that overshadows it is an ancient yew, believed to be more than 1,300 years old, from which the bowmen of Martindale took wood to make their weapons during the War of the Roses.

At its foot is the tomb – which I found after much searching – of the Rev Richard Birkett, the church's first resident priest, who served for an impressive 66 years before, on Christmas Day 1699, he died, leaving a bequest of £100 towards the continued service of his 'godly, sober and religious' successors.

Just up the hill from the Old Church, and almost within sight of it, is the New Church, St Peter's.

This was built in the early 1880s thanks to two local landowners – both members of the Parkin family – who provided the money, though why they felt the need to build another church when there was a very nice one just down the road is something I have been unable to establish.

Parkin – and, specifically, William Hugh Parkin, since that is the name bestowed upon each generation's firstborn male – is a name you see almost wherever you look in these parts, and memorials to various of them and their wealthy family abound around the church.

The most poignant – not least because I have since discovered that his grandson is a friend of mine (who turns out to be William Hugh Parkin the Seventh) – is that which commemorates the life of Lt Cdr William Hugh Parkin (the Fifth), a wartime naval pilot who died aged 33 in one of the biggest mysteries of World War II.

He was one of the 1,519 men who died when the aircraft carrier HMS Glorious and two escorting destroyers were sunk off the coast of Norway by the German battle cruisers Scharnhorst and Gneisenau in June 1940.

Many people – not least Parkin's family – believe there was an official cover-up to hide what they claim was the litany of incompetence and subterfuge leading to the disaster.

What is known is that the Glorious left the relative safety of a convoy to sail home with the protection of just two destroyers, in contravention of the Admiralty's official policy of aircraft carriers always being escorted by four destroyers and a cruiser.

The official reason for the Glorious heading home was that she was short of fuel . . . but recent investigations have shown that she in fact had plenty and could have stayed much longer under the protection of the other ships.

The real one, many people believe, is that HMS Glorious's captain had fallen out with his senior flying officers and wanted to get home quickly to court martial them.

Whatever, HMS Glorious and her inadequate escort of HMS Ardent and HMS Acasta were attacked by the German fleet which, the Admiralty insist, nobody knew was in the area.

Nine hundred men survived the sinking and took to the life-rafts, but they were left to their fate in the bitterly cold waters and all but 41 died even though the cruiser HMS Devonshire was less than 50 miles away on a top secret mission under radio silence to evacuate the King of Norway.

A memorial to Parkin and the other officers and men of HMS Glorious now stands in the church that his ancestors built – a stained glass window showing an aerial view of the ship as it ploughs its way through the icy seas.

There is something especially moving about such a memorial to such a disaster in such a peaceful place as Martindale, which, for me anyway, seems to be so far away from the horrors of war.

14
Nibthwaite

I have a confession to make: I have never read any of Arthur Ransome's books.

This might seem a little strange, since as a child I was obsessed by the sea and anything to do with ships, dreamed only of joining the merchant navy and, as an avid reader, devoured anything that could feed my dreams.

But I looked down upon the works of old Arthur because he wrote about boats on lakes – not ships on the sea – and I had no interest in anything that did not have an engine and at least one funnel.

I have, though, now vowed to put that right and read at least one of his books . . . because this A-Z of the Lake District took me to Nibthwaite, a tiny village on the eastern shore of Coniston Water, where Ransome was inspired to write 'Swallows and Amazons' and all the other tales of a group of outdoorsy children having adventures loosely based on those enjoyed by the sons and daughters of a friend who lived just up the road.

Nibthwaite is far away from the hustle and bustle that threatens to ruin some other more favoured parts of the Lake District, and it is where the Ransome family used to spend their holidays in the 1880s and 1890s.

It is said that every year the family travelled there by train and cart from their home in Leeds, and on arrival young Arthur would dip his hands in the lake just to confirm that he was indeed back in the place he loved so much.

He learned to sail there, fished for perch and minnows and had picnics on one of the islands – all experiences that he used when he became a writer in later life.

Nibthwaite was then (and is now) the sort of place most Lake District tourists never find – especially those who arrive in anything bigger than the smallest kind of campervans – and indeed, because it can only be reached by a 'VERY narrow road' (and the VERY is almost always in capital letters), many of the online motorhome forums warn against going anywhere near it.

Having a Bongo, however, I had no reason to be deterred by such warnings, for it is small enough to be untroubled by the narrowness of a road, so I plotted a scenic route to reach it – approaching from the north, through a part of the Lake District that even I, who have lived there for 30 years, knew hardly at all.

Grasmere, Ambleside and Hawkshead were all places I was reasonably familiar with, but after that I was branching out into the unknown along a road that threatened to peter out in a succession of high hedges and sharp bends until it deposited me firmly in a Lake District I had never seen before. There before me, suddenly, as I descended the final hill, was the glistening outline of Coniston Water – a lake I knew well enough from the main road that runs along the other side, but which looked totally different from this one.

Once past Brantwood (once the home of artist, philosopher, philanthropist, social thinker and all round good egg John Ruskin) the road became steadily more of an adventure, sometimes dodging around a rocky crag and sometimes almost seeming to be about to fall into the water, and I could understand why motorhomers were so regularly warned away from it.

I was close enough to Nibthwaite by then, so started looking for any potential overnight parking spaces and there were, to my surprise, several – two 'proper' car parks, nicely levelled and well off the road, and several more gateways in which a Bongo could happily be parked.

Any one of them would have done, and done quite well, but none promised the sheer perfection of the little quarry that I found – only a little bigger than a Bongo and dug into the cliff at the side of the road – which afforded the sort of views that have adorned many a calendar over the years.

Parked there, looking out onto the lake just a handful of metres away, with the evening sun shining gold on the water and three ducks paddling nonchalantly in the shallows, I could well understand what Arthur Ransome saw in the place.

All at once I became a Ransome devotee – an ignorant one, it's true, but one who wanted to follow in his footsteps all the same.

I was aware that I had passed the Swallow and Amazons Tearoom (closed) further up the road and I had passed too – hidden away somewhere in the trees on my left – the house in which in 1943 he wrote his last Lakeland book.

And I knew that Peel Island, which became Wild Cat Island in his books, was almost literally within a stone's throw from where I was parked, though it was hidden behind the attractive little tree-covered promontory which my map told me was called Low Peel Near.

But there were other places I wanted to seek out.

Having established that this was the spot in which I wanted to spend the night – and being fairly confident that, since it was out of season nobody else would have the same idea because any other tourists would be confined to the more populated side of the lake – I drove half a mile down the road into Nibthwaite village, where, my map told me, a short path led through a gate and into the field from which a famous ancient wharf jutted into the lake.

This – so the little research I had done told me – was the jetty, known as Slate Quay, that featured in several of his Ransome's books, so I felt obliged to take a look.

In any other place in the Lake District there would have been a pay-and-display car park. And at the very least an information panel, and maybe even a visitor centre too, telling me everything I needed to know about Arthur Ransome and his connection with the area.

But this was Nibthwaite – quiet, ignored and gloriously unspoiled Nibthwaite – and there was nothing at all, except a footpath sign and a hand-painted notice telling me to keep to the wall and not to walk across the middle of the field.

There was not anywhere I could reasonably park, so I tucked the Bongo as safely as I could beside an ancient barn and prayed that no farmer would come along in a tractor because if he did he would have trouble squeezing through the space I had left him.

But even at the risk of causing a modicum of traffic chaos I was determined to walk to the jetty – since it had clearly meant so much to my new hero.

The first surprise came just inside the gate, where I spotted the figure of a man – a sculpture by Antony Gormley (he of Angel of the North fame) – gazing out, as if looking for a friend who might be arriving by boat from the far side of the lake.

Exactly what such a thing was doing standing in a remote field looking out over a Cumbrian lake I had no idea – and it's something I have not been able to discover since. But sure enough it was there, unsung, unsignposted and unexplained . . . just three of the reasons I loved it.

It was a matter of a few more yards before I reached the jetty. Having never read his stories, I had no reason to think it, but even so I thought it looked every inch like something out of an Arthur

Ransome book – a little stone jetty reaching out from a green wooden boathouse, inside which a small white wooden boat was almost hidden.

A 'Private, Keep Out' sign reminded me that, Arthur Ransome or no, this was a place in which visitors like me were tolerated rather than encouraged, so I returned to the Bongo happy both that I had seen such an iconic place and, from the absence of cursing farm folk, that I had managed to do it without bringing the village's traffic to a standstill while I did so.

That evening I felt the need to go to the pub – and not only because it boasted of being one of Arthur's favourite drinking places.

The Red Lion is in Lowick, the next village down the valley from Nibthwaite. It is, I was pleased to discover, one of those pubs that oozes friendliness as soon as you open its door.

As I walked in the landlord smiled and said hello, the barmaid, who I took to be his wife, smiled, two men on stools at the bar smiled and nodded a welcome and an elderly couple sitting at a table beside the fireplace smiled.

No wonder Ransome liked coming here, I thought.

I bought a pint and at the landlord's suggestion sat down at a table on the other side of the fireplace from the couple to await the lasagne I had ordered.

Harry, the male half of the elderly couple, had his back to me but quickly swivelled on his chair for a small-talk chat about the joys of open fires, and within a few minutes Janine, his wife, saw that we were getting on well enough to invite me to join them at their table.

Janine and Harry were the sort of couple a stranger hopes to meet when he walks into a pub far from home.

I had soon learned their biographies (she was 80 years old, a retired physiotherapist, and he, a retired policeman, was, she said, her 69-year-old toyboy) just as they had soon learned mine.

They shared a love of motorbikes (hers, she said, had always been more powerful than his) and had been married for something over 20 years, though neither of them could remember just how long that something was. They lived several miles away on the other side of the lake and were only in the pub because they had had to take their dog to the vet and thought they might as well make a day of it.

Harry was delighted to hear that I was enjoying exploring Nibthwaite's local history – though Arthur Ransome was not what he had in mind.

The *really* interesting thing about the village, he told me, was the part it had played in the area's copper mining industry.

For many centuries the hills around Coniston had been famous for their huge deposits of copper, and in the days before railways the ore was taken to a wharf at Coniston village, loaded onto boats and transported to Nibthwaite at the far end of the lake before being taken the few miles overland to ships at Greenodd.

I would, if I had known what I was looking at, have seen the remains of the old warehouses near the jetty I had seen earlier in the afternoon, he told me.

We all left the pub together, they to their little cottage with its open fire and I to my handy parking place under the stars beside the lake.

And, like everyone I had met in the pub, I was smiling.

By the time the sun came up next morning I had decided upon my plan of action.

I would combine with my drive home a quick tour of a few more places associated with Arthur Ransome.

In another, even more commercialised and tourist-conscious world, such a tour would already exist – with helpful guidebooks, signposts and lay-bys at every place of interest. There are, after all, already Shakespeare, Thomas Hardy

But to celebrate the life of Arthur Ransome . . . there is, happily, nothing at all apart from a road atlas and the imagination of anyone reading it.

My route took me a few miles south from Nibthwaite, past Lowick Hall, which he rented for a while, and on over the hills to Low Ludderburn, where I searched in vain for the grey barn in which he wrote 'Swallows and Amazons' in a purpose-built first-floor writing room.

From there I drove to the village of Haverthwaite and his last Cumbrian home, known as Hill Top, and its wonderful views across the River Leven, and on to Rusland to find the little church in whose graveyard he and his wife Evgenia are buried.

Even as nothing more than a drive through beautiful countryside it would have been a superb journey, but the knowledge that I was following in the footsteps of Arthur Ransome, a great writer who loved this land so much, added great and special interest.

By the time I pulled up outside the little church on top of the hill, I felt that – even without reading any of his books – I knew the old chap better and was halfway to understanding him.

That feeling blossomed as I found my way to his grave. There was no signpost pointing the way, no glossy explanatory leaflet, no heap of admirers' flowers, not even a rough footpath made by the feet of legions of his fans. Just a plain, square, granite block with the words:

ARTHUR RANSOME
Born 18 January 1884
Died 3 June 1967
and his wife
EVGENIA RANSOME
Born 10 April 1894
Died 12 March 1973

No mention, you will note, of his ever having been one of the greatest writers of his generation. No mention that he was anyone out of the ordinary at all.

And certainly no mention that he was a spy.

But it is pretty widely accepted now that that is indeed what he was, at least for a part of his life.

There were, it seems, three Arthur Ransomes.

There was the little boy playing with his friends and siblings, and learning how to sail boats and make picnics while on holiday at Nibthwaite.

There was the middle-aged man – bald and besporting a moustache so droopy he looked like a walrus – who moved back to the area so he could write his books.

And in between there was a man so radical that he was suspected – maybe rightly – of being a Russian agent.

It was in 1913 that Ransome, by then a successful journalist, first moved to Russia – though there was always the suspicion that he only did it to escape from his first wife Ivy, because he knew she did not have the necessary passport to follow him there

When the First World War broke out, Arthur became a war correspondent (his ill health and poor eyesight ruled him out of being called up to fight) and when in 1917 the Russian Revolution erupted he found himself firmly on the side of the Bolsheviks.

There is no doubt that at that time he was being employed as a secret agent by the British government, but that did not stop him numbering Lenin and Trotsky among his friends.

Nor, it was suspected, did it stop him passing information to them.

His name appeared in top secret MI5 files on people and organisations involved in espionage during the First World War, and he was arrested as a security risk on one of his returns to London, but whether or not he really was a spy is debatable.

There is no doubting that his love for Trotsky's secretary Evgenia Shelepina was genuine enough, though. He married her, and eventually moved with her back to England – and his beloved Lake District – and she is, as we have seen, buried alongside him in the churchyard at Rusland.

Ransome, it is said, asked to be buried at Rusland because it was the most peaceful place he knew, and as I stood at his grave I understood.

And I realised something that was as thrilling as it was unexpected.

There was not a sound.

Just to make sure, I stopped breathing.

And, holding my breath for a moment, I knew I was right: No human voices, no mooing cows or bleating sheep, no birds, no distant tractors, not even the gentle rustling of grass in the breeze. Nothing.

Rusland church, where Arthur Ransome now lies, is indeed one of the most peaceful places on earth.

15
Overwater

Overwater is somewhere that most people who visit the Lake District (and even some who live there) will have never heard of.

It is only five miles from Keswick, but is as far removed from the bustle of that tidy little town as it is possible to imagine.

Indeed, it is not really a place at all. It's a tiny lake, set in a valley between Skiddaw and Binsey, and at the foot of a winding road that leads down from the glorious wildness of Caldbeck Common, and it has absolutely no facilities for the tourist apart from a small sign proclaiming it to be owned by the National Trust.

The land around it is the property of an assortment of local landowners who have never seen the need to get together to create a round-the-lake footpath for the few visitors who might appreciate it and the only concessions to tourism I have ever been able to find is a small car park – big enough for no more than five vehicles – and a there-and-back footpath leading the 100 metres from it to the water's edge.

What it does have – and what made it an inviting location when I came to organising my Lake District A-Z – is an unassuming natural beauty . . . and a jaw-dropping history of violent death.

It is little more than a half-hour drive from my house, so, knowing that a pub, cafe or any form of late-night entertainment was out of the question in such a place, I made up the bed in the Bongo and put on my pyjamas (I actually wear an old tracksuit, but let's not be pedantic) before leaving home.

It was, after all, midwinter and it had already been dark and freezing for several hours.

The little car park that I was aiming for was, happily, empty when I arrived, so I parked among the puddles in the dark, climbed into the back and settled down for a quiet night.

And quiet it was. With only one passing car all night, it was one of my most peaceful Bongo Nights ever.

The trouble was it was also one of the coldest.

By the small hours of the morning I was dressed in every item of clothing I had – in addition to the pyjamas I had on when I went to bed, I now was wearing my jeans, long-johns , a T-shirt, two sweaters and a fleece jacket – and, though wrapped tightly in the duvet and all the blankets I could find, still I was cold.

It was a long night.

But at least it meant I was awake to appreciate one of the finest and clearest starry nights I had ever seen, and – reckoning that going for a short walk around the car park in the small hours might at least get my circulation going long enough to offer some warmth – I twice left the van to stand among the puddles for a better look.

My plan for the morning was to walk around the lake (a combination of country lanes and footpaths meant it was possible to navigate a three-mile alternative to the lakeside path that the landowners had failed to come up with) and almost before it was light I had had my breakfast and was setting off into what promised to be a perfect day.

The hedges and verges were cloaked in white frost (no wonder I had been so cold) and the tarmac under my feet was so dangerously icy I walked at the pace of a very old man.

But what a magical morning it was!

The sun was already showing over the dark outline of the fells to the east, and the lake was bathed in the golden coat of winter light.

The lake is known as a favourite feeding place for the ospreys that famously nest just down the road on the other side of Bassenthwaite, but I knew it was too early in the year to see them, although I did spot a couple of buzzards already enjoying the early morning thermals.

And just a few minutes later, after finding myself in Orthwaite, a pretty village dominated by the pink painted Orthwaite Hall, a 16th century farmhouse which is a Grade II listed building, I discovered that buzzards too have something of a reputation in the area.

A stile to my right took me over a high wall above which a sign warned me of the danger of low flying buzzards which had been known to attack unsuspecting and unprepared walkers, and advised me to wear a hat and carry an umbrella to fend them off.

I confess I scoffed at that, dismissing it it as an unnecessary piece of alarmism and, no doubt, muttered something about the 'nanny state' . . . and anyway although I had no umbrella I felt safe enough under my favourite thickly-knitted woolly hat.

So far I had not seen or heard any sign of human life – something that continued as I followed the path around the southern end of the lake and into a field containing the impressive remains of an ancient earthwork.

Exactly what this ancient monument is, and indeed exactly how ancient it is, is a matter of some dispute.

Some, including the owners of the posh Overwater Hall – now a luxury hotel, but once a private house – which overlooks the lake, say it is what is left of a Roman army barracks.

'It is said that the area may have been used for the recreation and enjoyment of weary soldiers – perhaps those relieved from duty at other camps in the area, even from Hadrian's Wall itself,' they say on the hotel's website. 'This may be fanciful thinking, but if true it could be that people have been taking holidays at Overwater for almost two thousand years.'

Fanciful thinking, indeed, it seems.

For a more popular explanation these days – and one that is supported by Historic England – is that the banks and ditches are in fact all that's left of a medieval mansion, possibly even the original Overwater Hall.

The argument over the monument does nothing to spoil Overwater's claim to bloody notoriety.

For there is no dispute at all that here was the scene of a particularly gruesome murder at the start of the 19th century.

The sorry saga involved one Joseph Gillbanks, who – as a prosperous, genteel, well respected and fine upstanding citizen who'd made his fortune as a merchant trader in Jamaica – returned to Britain with his wife in 1814.

He bought Overwater Hall, had his family motto, Honore et Virtute (that's honour and courage to you and me) carved above its front door, became a magistrate and in all respects set about living the life of the local squire that he aspired to be.

Who would have guessed that he had a guilty secret in the shape of a young black woman . . . or that she would hitch a lift on a steamer from the West Indies and turn up on his Cumbrian doorstep demanding a little financial help to look after the child he had fathered during their clandestine affair during his time in the Caribbean all those years before?

Gillbanks, while pretending to welcome her into his comfortable new life, took her out for a trip in his boat on the lake at the bottom of his garden . . . and threw her overboard.

To his dismay she could swim, or float well enough to try to climb back on board anyway, so he dragged her back onto the boat, chopped off her arms with his sword, dispatched her back into the water and saw that this time she sank as intended.

He returned to the Hall – and to his wife – to continue his life as a successful local dignitary and, though his crime is thought to have been pretty common knowledge among the few people who made up the local community, nothing more was said.

Gilbanks was never charged with murder or, as far as we know, ever even questioned about it, so when he died it was in his own bed, aged 73 and still the epitome of the respected country squire.

119

That, so legend tells us, was not the end of it, though.

For, we hear, the poor girl has returned to haunt the Hall ever since.

She has kept coming back there in ghostly form, so scaring the wits out of the staff working there that they refused to sleep in the servants' quarters on the top floor – which is why a cluster of little cottages had to be built especially for them just down the road.

In the years since it became a hotel, guests and staff have continued to report seeing the ghost of a black girl with no arms stalking the corridors and, we are told, Overwater tarn has never frozen over because, even in the coldest winter, a black hand and arm has been seen pushing through to break up the ice.

That, you might think, would be enough for any historic mansion to boast about, but Overwater Hall has another claim to notoriety.

This involves one Charles Norman de Courcy-Parry, the wayward son of the Chief Constable of Cumberland, who lived there in the 1950s and, by coincidence, happens to be one of the people who claimed to have seen the armless ghost.

He had, it seems led quite a life.

In a later magazine interview he described how he had 'fought in two great wars, battled in a South-American revolution, worked a passage around the world, fought in the ring for the Middleweight Championship of French Oceania, been a ship's cook, a swagman in Australia, a Master of Foxhounds, travelled alone behind the Iron Curtain. . . and been in jail too'.

What he did not say is that there is a good chance that he was also the man who shot and killed Percy Toplis.

Toplis was an army deserter from the First World War and an alleged murderer who became famous a few years ago when the BBC called him 'The Monocled Mutineer' and made a TV series about him.

He had been at the centre of the British Army mutiny at an infamous and brutal training base in Flanders, and was at the time the most wanted man in the country.

When, after a nationwide hunt, Toplis turned up at Plumpton, near Penrith, the 22-year-old de Courcy-Parry joined his father's police

posse, taking with him the small Belgian automatic pistol that he had pocketed as an unofficial souvenir from the war.

The actual circumstances of what happened next are still a mystery. Toplis was certainly shot dead, and the young de Courcy-Parry, leading the police chase on his 1,000cc American motorcycle, is generally thought to have been the man who fired the fatal bullet.

Such violence seemed to be a million miles away as I continued my walk on the Overwater byways. The path took me around the perimeter of the earthwork and onto a muddy track that skirted the grounds of the hotel (I might have gone in for a coffee, but there was no sign that either I or my muddy boots would be welcome in such an establishment) and out onto the road that skirted the northern side of the tarn.

After the quietness of my night there I was surprised by the number of cars using such an out-of-the way thoroughfare, and even more surprised when I got back to my parking place to find that the Bongo was now surrounded by four other cars, one of which – with an elderly couple sitting inside – was blocking my way out.

The driver quickly gave me a cheery smile and a gesture of apology and started his engine, moving forward just far enough to allow the

Bongo to squeeze past. I smiled back and thanked him for his thoughtfulness.

'The ice on your windows tells me you spent the night here,' he said, dragging himself out of his car. 'Must've been lovely.'

'Lovely,' I agreed. 'But absolutely bloody freezing.'

He told me that he lived on the other side of the Lake District, at Parton, near the coast, but he and his wife often drove the 20 miles to Overwater because it was one of their favourite places and where they had liked to walk before she became too infirm to get out of the car.

He told me that one of his favourite walks had been the one around the lake and I told him that was the one I was just finishing.

'The buzzards didn't get you, then?'

I told him I had seen the warning sign but had assumed it was just a piece of health-and-safety nonsense.

'Not at all . . . and I've got the scars to prove it!'

My new friend whipped off his cap and proudly pointed towards an inch-long pink blemish on his bald head.

'It just swooped down out of nowhere,' he said. 'I tried to use my walking stick but I wasn't quick enough. Savage, it was.'

16
Pooley Bridge

The woman in the pub looked perplexed as she nursed her large glass of house red wine.

'Do you know how far Ullswater is from here?' she asked.

'About 200 metres,' I replied.

And now she looked surprised.

'Really? You're kidding me. Two hundred metres? I thought it was at least another 20 miles!'

The woman and her son – an astrophysics student who'd taken the weekend off from university for a weekend with his mum – were at the Sun Inn in Pooley Bridge for exactly the same reason as I was: It was one of those enlightened pubs known to allow campervans to spend the night in their car parks.

We had both arrived there in the dark, had both parked our vans in dark corners of the car park, had both promised the landlord we would spend money in his pub in return for his hospitality and were both now proving it by passing the evening supping at his bar.

The big difference between me and her was that, while I knew the area – and therefore knew precisely where Ullswater was – she had not even bothered to look at a map to find out.

All she cared about was having somewhere – anywhere – to spend the night.

Even so, there is a certain camaraderie between owners of campervans, and not surprisingly it took no time at all for me to wangle myself a look at hers.

What a surprise it was! On the outside it looked like any other old white Ford Transit – a plumber's maybe, or a small-time builder's doing odd jobs for pensioners – but inside it was anything but.

The windowless walls were hung with thick drapes in a paintbox of blues, greens and deep pinks; a discreet string of fairylights twinkled against the deep purple sheet that billowed from the roof; a full-sized double bed managed to hide itself beneath an array of colourful throws and cushions; and somewhere among it all was squeezed all the other paraphernalia – gas stove, larder, cooking utensils and big plastic boxes that doubled as a wardrobe and, when upturned, seats – that any campervan needs.

'That's beautiful,' I told her. 'I could never have guessed.'

'Quite bordello-ish,' she laughed.

'Yes, but a very lovely bordello.'

It seemed that my new friends had simply followed their satnav to the Sun Inn, knowing nothing about it – least of all where it was – other than that they would be able to park their van there, so, even though it was dark, I thought it only polite to grab my torch and offer them a guided tour of the village.

As we walked down the main street I described how all the properties there had been wrecked by the floods wrought by Storm Desmond a few years before, how the village had been virtually cut off for weeks and how my wife and I had shed tears when we heard that the wonderful old stone bridge that had given Pooley Bridge its name had been washed away by the force of the water.

We found our way down a pitch dark footpath to the shore, and listened to the waves gently whispering on the stones at our feet.

I shone my little torch (gratifyingly bright for one that cost a mere £1.89 from Sainsbury's) out into the distance, where the glistening surface of the lake could just about be made out.

'There you are – now you've seen Ullswater,' I said. 'Two hundred metres, like I said.'

They were up early next morning – I heard their van pulling out of the car park while I was still in bed – so I had no chance to say goodbye. But they sent me a message later telling me that they had made it to Windermere and that they had followed my advice and gone via the western shore of Ullswater, through Glenridding and Patterdale, and over the 'pretty hairy' Kirkstone Pass to Ambleside.

My own day was spent much more locally and – some would say – much less adventurously.

The obvious thing to do when staying in Pooley Bridge is to walk towards Ullswater, and catch a boat or maybe climb one of the hills – Heughscar on one side, or Little Mell Fell on the other – which afford famously fine views over the lake and the mountains beyond.

But I am not one to do the obvious.

I intended to walk in precisely the opposite direction – a gentle five-mile ramble down the River Eamont to the tiny settlement of Barton, where a splendid 12th century church stands in a circular churchyard among some of the most unspoiled farmland you will find anywhere in Britain, and then up to the lower slopes of the fells and round through more farmland back to Pooley Bridge.

And I planned to add some spice to it by inviting to accompany me my friend Mark Richards – a fellwalker and guidebook writer famous for his books on the highest of the Lake District mountains who, I knew, would normally look upon such a 'stroll' as being barely worth his attention.

Many keen fell walkers, I know, display a certain snobbery in regard to their sport ('the arrogance of the fell walker' is a phrase given to me by a non-walking friend, when we were discussing the phenomenon later). They make it clear that they believe any sort of walking which does not involve full mountain gear, walking poles, a day's supply of emergency rations and the potential need to call upon the services of Mountain Rescue isn't really walking at all.

Their way of enjoying the Lake District is, in their book, the only way . . . and anyone (like me) who chooses some other way is not to be bothered with.

Mark is, I'm happy to say, not one of them – and when he sometimes ventures too close to expressing that point of view he is man enough to admit it and to join in the laughter when I tease him about it.

On this occasion I was determined, if not to introduce him to the joys of low-level walking, then at least to remind him that you don't have to slog 1,000 metres up a hill to have an enjoyable and fulfilling day out in the Lake District.

Mark and Helen joined me for my now usual breakfast of ham, cheese and chutney tortilla in the Bongo before he and I set off through the pub car park and onto the well made up path beside the river.

It is the sort of walk that, inevitably, is popular with dog owners . . . and which, therefore, is frequently decorated by the plastic bags of poo they see fit to leave hanging from the trees, fences and gateposts.

'How would you like it if I bagged my sheep shit and hung it from your garden fence or gate?' said a sign that greeted us after a few yards.

Fair enough, I thought . . .

Walking with Mark is an experience like no other!

I like to think I am pretty observant (and I did spot an impressive lime kiln that he walked right past, unseeing) but he sees – and knows about – things that seem to be of little interest until he points them out and starts talking about them.

'That hill on the left is Dunmallard, which most people think must be something to do with ducks,' he told me as we got into our stride. 'But it was originally known as Dunmallet or Dun Malloch.

'You probably know there's an ancient earthwork on the top – that's where the "Dun" comes from, meaning a hill fort, as in Dundee.

'But did you know it's the scene of some sort of battle, whose details are long lost in the mists of time? That's the "Malloch", or skirmish. So Dun Malloch was the hill fort where the skirmish was.'

'Nothing to do with ducks?' I asked.

'Nothing.'

We came to a farm.

'Look closely at the concrete in the farmyard and you'll find dozens of chickens' footprints. It seems that the flock went for a walk before the concrete was dry.'

And when we chanced upon an interesting looking piece of machinery left to rust in a field I thought it was probably something to turn over hay left to dry in the sun but . . .

'It's an old horse-drawn potato-lifter,' said Mark. 'Those spikey wheels would dig into the ground as they were spinning, so digging up all the spuds. Then someone would just have to follow along behind and pick them up. Probably about the 1920s, I should think.'

We came to a lovely view over the river.

'Somewhere along here – nobody is quite sure – is where the United Kingdom first became united,' Mark told me.

'All we really know is that it was somewhere along the River Eamont, so it could have been at this very spot just as likely as anywhere else.

'All the kings of Britain – people like Constantin of Scotland, Owain of Strathclyde and Hywel Dda, King of Wales were all brought together by Athelstan of England in the year 927 to agree a truce, presumably to form some sort of coalition against the Vikings.

'It was known as the Eamont Treaty because it happened somewhere along this stretch of the river, but nobody knows exactly where so we might as well say it was here.'

We came to the remains of a Roman road, which I knew to be part of High Street, the route that in days long gone by ran across the fells to link the settlements that became Ambleside and Penrith,

'Of course, most of High Street wasn't really Roman at all,' Mark told me. 'It was much older than that. Ancient peoples had been using it for centuries before the Romans came along.'

Mark seemed to be enjoying the walk even though, being only 900 metres above sea level at its highest point it was, by his standards, a pretty tame affair.

All I was hoping for was some special place, some moment of magic, to encapsulate why I enjoy such adventures as much as I do.

As we climbed a hill so gentle that neither of us had to slow down, let alone pause for breath, I was praying that once at the top we would be faced with a view so magnificent that even Mark would be lost for words.

The view from the top was, shall we say, disappointing, but we only had to walk a few more paces to be faced with exactly what I was hoping for.

The sun broke through, the sky was suddenly blue and the clouds pure white, and ahead of us stretched the whole of Ullswater, with the ragged outline of the Helvellyn range in the distance.

And, to cap it all, we saw that the tops of those fells were all encased in a thick, unpleasant-looking mist.

'Now, Mark,' I said, barely able to keep the smug chuckle from my voice, 'just look at that. Isn't that just wonderful? Just perfect? If I hadn't persuaded you to come walking with me you'd have been up there in those clouds and you wouldn't be able to see a thing. No sunshine. No blue sky. No view.'

He muttered something. But he didn't seem to be convinced.

17
Quaker Hill

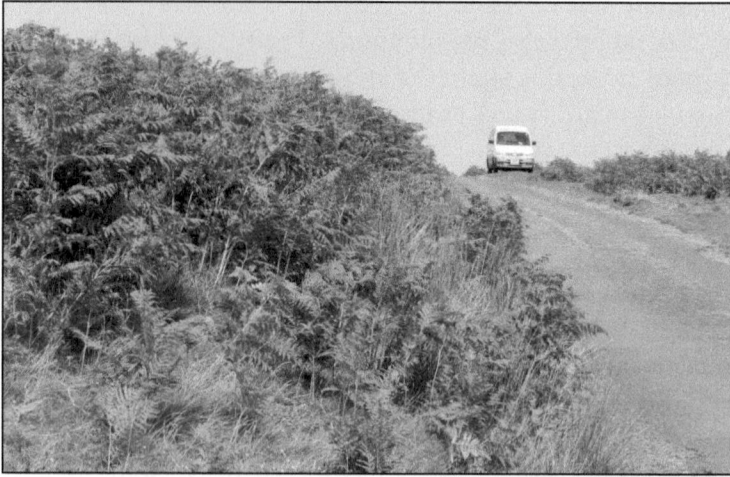

Some places are just made to be woken up in by an old man in a campervan. Some quiet, out-of-the-way spot overlooking a little harbour, maybe; or a patch of stubbly grass beside the tumbling waters of a wild mountain stream.

Or perhaps a remote clifftop looking out over nothing but hundreds of miles of sea.

Or some peaceful hideaway on the side of a hill, where all is pitch dark and silent until the sun begins to rise over the hills in the distance and sends its golden early morning light through the chink in the curtain and starts to warm up the slopes of the magnificent mountains which lie at the bottom end of the valley.

It was in just such a place that I managed to complete the 17th night of my A-Z of the Lake District.

Q was always going to be difficult.

Places beginning with Q are hard to find in Cumbria. In fact there is, as far as I could tell, only one – Quality Corner, a hamlet a mile or so inland from the port of Whitehaven, which, because it lies outside the National Park, did not qualify under the rules I had set myself.

I was beginning to despair, and thinking of clever ways to get around the problem (I thought perhaps the Quiet Site, a campsite near Ullswater, and someone suggested I could sit in a queue of traffic heading to Bowness-on-Windermere on a Bank Holiday Monday).

And then fate – or good fortune, anyway – took a hand.

Tricia was planning to go for a walk with a friend, up a mountain called High Pike, along a route with which neither she nor I was familiar.

I looked at the map of the area on the OS app on my mobile, then zoomed in to get a bigger-scale picture of the place where she was planning to park her car.

And there, right next to her proposed parking spot, was . . . Quaker Hill.

Quaker Hill, a hill so small it hardly deserves the title; unnamed on most maps and too insignificant to be known by even the most knowledgeable of my fell-walking friends. A hill on the western side of the Caldew valley, which runs south-to-north between the villages of Mosedale and Hesket Newmarket, beneath the towering gaze of Carrock Fell towards the northern fringes of the National Park.

My plan was to park there, facing east, so that I would catch the sun as it rose over Cross Fell and the Pennine hills in the distance in front of me, sending golden rays over the breathtaking view of Helvellyn, Great Mell Fell and High Street closer, to my right.

And parking there in the quiet beauty of such a place was everything I had hoped for . . . except that by the time I woke up the sun was long past rising and the whole valley was bathed in the bright sunshine of what turned out to be a glorious day.

Never has a Bongo breakfast (my usual ham, cheese and chutney in a quickly heated tortilla) been eaten in such a splendidly scenic – and sunny – location.

It took all of five minutes to reach the top of Quaker Hill. A hundred metres or so up the track Tricia had taken to High Pike, then a dive off to the right for an easy walk through the bracken to what I judged to be the highest point.

There is, apparently, no known link between Quaker Hill and Quakerism – even though this part of Cumbria was a centre of the movement in the 17th century, and one of its last remaining Friends Meeting Houses is still very active in the village of Mosedale just a mile down the road.

I had taken the trouble to email the local Friends, asking if they knew why the hill had been so named, but the answer was that they knew of no reason at all.

Even so, I had got it into my head that Quaker Hill was so named because it was where the early Quakers held their open air meetings in the years before the Mosedale Meeting House was built, and I was not going to change my mind just because there was no evidence to prove it.

Certainly as I stood on the top of the hill I could believe that this was where the devout believers of 350 years ago would have met to praise their god.

If I were to believe in a god, standing there with the majesty of his creation laid out before me would be enough to make me sing his name to the heavens.

And – was it just my mind and my heart playing tricks? – there was something deeply spiritual about the place.

Just like the feeling I get when I am all alone in some ancient site – a prehistoric stone circle, say, or a stone age burial mound or a magnificent 12th century cathedral – I felt something.

I have no idea what. But definitely something.

And I was more convinced than ever that, no matter what the history books said, or didn't say, Quaker Hill had, at some time in the past, been a place of great religious meaning and sacred importance.

Mosedale is a mere mile-long stroll away, along the road, but it's a road that's always busy with traffic so I took the lazy way out and drove.

I had already worked out a circular walk – parking just outside the village, then walking to the Friends Meeting House, before heading off down a farm track to the River Caldew, before returning to the Bongo via an attractive looking route through fields and country lanes.

The Meeting House, and indeed the whole idea of Quakerism, has interested – almost enchanted – me for years.

If I was going to be anything, I tell people, I would be a Quaker, if only because their 'services' consist of sitting around in silence until someone feels moved to say something.

It's a movement that was founded by one George Fox, a weaver's son from Leicestershire, who used his uncompromising approach to Christianity to rebel against both the religious and political authorities embodied by Oliver Cromwell. in the mid 1600s.

He travelled all over the country, preaching sermons of dissent, and was jailed numerous times for his beliefs.

Those travels inevitably took him to Cumbria, and he found a particular welcome there, especially in the areas around Cockermouth and, later, Mosedale, and in 1650 – three years after he started his mission – he attracted huge crowds to his meetings, frequently held in the open air, at some prominent local beauty spot.

Fox visited Mosedale in 1653, though there is no evidence that (as I like to believe) he preached on top of Quaker Hill while he was there.

Even so Quakerism gained an enthusiastic following in the Mosedale valley, with meetings for worship taking place in a private house until in 1702 a Meeting House was set up in an old barn.

From then on it was steadily improved and converted, so that it became the fine, atmospheric Meeting House that it is today.

I first found the Mosedale Meeting House many years ago, just when I was beginning my spell as a freelance journalist, having been sacked after three inglorious years as editor of the local papers in Carlisle.

I visited it after persuading the Daily Express to use a feature I had written, about the Meeting House and the way volunteer Quakers turned it into a tea shop in the summer – which if nothing else gave me an excuse for a day out in the Lake District, even though the fee I was paid barely justified the time and trouble I devoted to it.

Still, I remember it as a beautifully dignified place, offering a wonderfully calm and comforting haven from the commercialism of the Lake District, even despite the hubbub of conversation and clatter of teacups.

When I returned for my Bongo Night I was disappointed to find the Meeting House was closed.

But there was still plenty to enjoy . . . and it was clear I was welcome to enjoy it.

A gate beside the building led into a small garden, which a sign told me: 'We are happy to allow quiet enjoyment of this Garth.'

I sat there for many minutes, simply enjoying the peace that seems to emanate from the place.

And I sat too in another garden – across the road, next to the Meeting House car park in which, another friendly sign told me, I was welcome to park my car.

This was a peace garden, a former burial ground, where now a few simple benches provide visitors with the opportunity to spend a few moments in quiet thought.

Dragging myself away from the garden, I found myself walking a short distance on the road through the pretty village before branching off onto a farm track leading away from the higher ground towards the flatlands of the valley through which the River Caldew was making its stately progress towards Carlisle and the sea.

A family were enjoying a swim there, in a surprisingly deep pool under a footbridge, and I guessed (correctly, as they told me) that they were locals because nobody could have chanced upon such a remote place without a good deal of local knowledge.

In fact one of the joys of this part of the Lake District is that most tourists don't chance upon it either.

It is well off the beaten track that leads to such hotspots as Ambleside, Keswick or Bowness-on-Windermere, and has few attractions other than the scenery, and no facilities at all apart from a couple of pubs and an often deserted Quaker Meeting House.

But what more, I wondered as I walked across a field with the Bongo in sight, does anyone really need?

18
Rydal

There was a place in the Lake District that I had tried many times to find.

But though I had often been to Rydal Water before, and had walked around it several times and had had more than one picnic on its shores, I had never been able to locate it: The Rydal Cave.

I had already earmarked a suitable overnight Bongo spot – close to (but not blocking) a cattle grid on a very minor no-through-road that led only to a couple of B&Bs off the main route to Ambleside.

It did not matter that when I got there I found someone else had had the same idea (an old VW campervan was already there, and by the look of it was unlikely to be leaving at any time soon) so I paid to park in a National Park car park just up the road instead and postponed finding an overnight parking spot until later.

My plan was to walk along the popular path on the south side of Rydal Water, but this time to walk slower than my usual pace so I had time to look out for the fingerpost which, I was confident, would divert me to wherever the cave might be.

I had looked at the map on my smartphone, of course – the Ordnance Survey app is surely one of the best innovations of recent years – and had blown it up to its maximum extent so I could see the area in greatest detail.

But I had been surprised to find no sign of any symbol denoting a cave.

No matter, I thought, I would be sure to find it if, remembering my past failures, this time I kept my eyes open.

The path along the lake was as perfect as I remembered – an easy stroll on a mostly well made path just a few feet from the water.

The sun was shining, the sky was blue, a few mute swans dabbed away on the far side of the lake and a single red breasted merganser kept a careful watch over me on mine, and there was hardly a sound apart from the water rippling gently against the pebbles on the beaches.

I was in a world of my own – and what a lovely world it was! – and I had reached the far end of the lake before I realised I had, yet again, failed to find the cave.

I was confident that I had not missed a signpost to it, nor failed to notice any well worn paths up to where it must be.

It was a mystery . . . created, I had little doubt, by my own incompetence.

I wandered, just a little annoyed with myself, up to the main lakeside car park where, I guessed, the inevitable map for visitors would be standing helpfully beside the pay-and-display machine to tell me where the cave was.

It did. The cave – or, rather 'caves' (I had no idea there was more than one) – were shown to be on a path running almost parallel, but higher up the hill, to the one I had taken beside the lake.

I turned back and retraced my steps – noting that from this car park the caves were indeed signposted.

Half a mile on and I came upon a crossroads of footpaths.

To the left, a fingerpost told me, was Rydal village; to the right was Grasmere.

And straight on was another path, muddier than the others and heading uphill, which was not signposted at all.

This, I reckoned by process of elimination, must lead to the cave.

I slogged my way up through the mud, nearly slipping and landing on my back several times, until I reached a plateau where the path diverted sharply to the left.

A young couple were taking a breather on a rock.

'Any idea where this famous cave is?' I asked.

The boy looked at me vacantly, then pulled the headphones from his ears.

'Eh?'

'Any idea where this famous cave is?'

'We're hoping it's just around this next bend,' he told me in an accent whose plumminess took me by surprise. 'That's what our map seems to be signifying, anyway.'

I thanked him, wished him a happy walk and went on my way – wondering not just why his map marked the cave while mine did not, but also what sort of man it was who felt the need for music in his ears when he went for a romantic walk in a place like this with his lovely girlfriend.

The cave was, as he had said, just around the next bend.

And it was much more impressive than anything I had been expecting.

It was huge – a great open archway leading, it seemed, into the very heart of the mountain – and as I walked gingerly over the line of stepping stones that led across the little lake at the entrance (a lake which, it is claimed, even includes goldfish among the myriad small species swimming in it) it was like walking into the mouth of a whale.

Rydal Cave is, of course, not a natural one – it's just one of the many relics of the slate quarries that still scar these hills from long ago – but it's none the less dramatic for that and being right inside it, pressed in the dark against the rock in its deepest recesses, it truly does feel as if you've somehow entered into an undiscovered world.

After so many failed attempts to find it, I felt an absurd degree of satisfaction and fetched a ham sandwich from my rucsac to celebrate.

I took another look at my mobile, stupidly checking that the cave had not somehow appeared on my OS map on my trek up to it.

I was right, my OS map, for all its tiny detail, failed to mention the cave.

I switched it back to its normal scale . . . and the word 'cave' magically jumped onto the page, just on the spot at which I was standing.

And there I had the explanation.

The digital version of the OS map for Rydal water does indeed tell you where the cave is . . . as long as you keep it to the standard scale. But if you zoom in, trying to get more detail, the cave disappears.

With my mission to find the cave safely behind me I set out to complete my walk around the lake (something I could have done in little more than an hour had I not spent so long getting lost).

It is a super walk – down one side, on the lakeside path, then through the White Moss car park, over the road and up to the old coffin route, along which mourners used to follow the funeral procession to St Oswald's Church in Grasmere.

From here there are wonderful views back down over the lake and the River Rothay, with rushing becks, tumbling waterfalls and ancient forests all in the space of not much more than a mile.

Towards the end a poster invited me to visit Rydal Hall and its 'open till 4pm' cafe.

Perfect I thought! A hot chocolate and a slice of carrot cake suddenly seemed overwhelmingly tempting.

Rydal Hall is a splendid 19th century arts and crafts mansion now owned by the Diocese of Carlisle and run as a retreat and holiday centre. It is set on a huge estate which has all the attractions you would associate with such a place – formal gardens, informal gardens, winding paths, woodland, ponds and a grotto.

It's the sort of beautiful place in which anyone after a bit of quiet and relaxation could spend a happy few hours.

And best of all, it's free.

A sign at the entrance invites visitors to 'just find a path and see where it leads', which I found enormously gratifying in a world in which there are not enough dos and too many don'ts.

The path I chose took me past the front of the house and up beside a stream to a mysterious little door that led, it seemed, into the side of the hill. I opened it and nearly fell over a row of yellow hard hats hanging on pegs just inside.

This was the ice house, a naturally cold place where ice was stored for the occupants of the big house in days gone by – an ice house dug so deep into the hillside that visitors these days need safety gear to explore it.

In other circumstances I would have taken up the unspoken invitation, but my mind was too set on hot chocolate to waste time on such fripperies.

I closed the door behind me and set off back down the hill towards the old schoolroom.

Unfortunately the warm feeling I had following my chosen path cooled a little when I discovered that the cafe upon which I had my sights – converted from an old school room that one of the early owners of the Hall had built for his son – was already closed.

Why, I wondered, keep a sign inviting visitors to take tea until 4pm when in fact they can't do it after 3pm?

Pure laziness, I suppose. And very irritating laziness at that!

I took my leave of Rydal Hall feeling not quite so well disposed towards it as I had been when I arrived.

By then I had decided where I would be spending the night.

On my walk through the White Moss car park I took the opportunity to confirm what several online camping guides had told me – unlike most of the car parks in the area it was owned by the Lowther Estate (one of the biggest private landowners in the Lake District) and unlike those run by the National Park it came with no regulations banning the overnight parking of campervans.

It did not offer splendid open views over lakes or mountains, it's true, but I knew that there among the trees, just a very short walk from Rydal Water, I would be safe and not unwelcome.

First though I had a call to make.

Being so close to it, I wanted to renew my acquaintance with the Unicorn pub – the very welcoming inn I had discovered on my visit to Ambleside on the very first night of my A-Z adventure.

I parked on the main street (being rewarded with a satisfying round of applause from a family standing watching on the pavement as I reversed into a tight space not very much longer than the Bongo itself) and set off for a night on the town.

Ambleside is a town that rewards a gentle evening stroll – lots of quaint streets, pretty slate-built houses, shops with their brightly lit windows full of all kinds of interesting things that I know I would never find a use for . . . and, on this day anyway, an almost total absence of people.

I wandered for an hour, going wherever the fancy took me, up this road, down that one, across to there and back to here and stopped only when a a heavy shower that I was not expecting sent me hurrying inside for shelter just as I was passing Zeffirellis cinema (the bigger brother of Fellinis, in which I had spent a blood thirsty couple of hours on my first trip).

I was just in time to catch the evening screening of '1917', the much vaunted film that everyone was talking about at that time (beautifully filmed and thought provoking, but totally implausible, if you want my opinion), which took me up to the time at which my stomach was feeling ready for my return visit to the Unicorn.

It was, I was happy to discover, just as welcoming as it had been six months previously.

The barman smiled, small-talked and suggested I might like to take a seat at the table which, by chance, was precisely the same as the one at which I had sat before.

A middle-aged couple on the next table smiled a greeting and suggested I should try the meatballs for which the Unicorn was famous.

'We've been coming here for 12 years and I always have the same thing,' the male half said.

'Just like we always stay in the same little cottage,' his wife added.

'And go on the same walks.'

I soon discovered that every year this couple, from Manchester, made a pilgrimage to Ambleside and had precisely the same holiday as they had had the year before, and the year before that, and the year ...

'You probably think it's boring. But we know what we like.'

I liked them, and they had offered me friendship, so I wasn't going to tell them what I really thought. Same cottage, same pub, same meatballs, same walks . . ?

'If it's what you like why change it?' I said with as much conviction as I could muster. 'At least you know you won't be disappointed.'

19
Scarness

Here is a good question for a pub quiz: How many lakes are there in the Lake District?

The answer – beloved of pedants like me – is: 'Just one.'

And that one is Bassenthwaite, near Keswick.

All the others are meres (Winder-, Gras-, Thirl- etc), waters (Ulls-, Brothers-, Derwent- Over- etc) or tarns (Loughrigg, Blea, Little Langdale etc) and to add the word 'lake' to their names is just an ignorant type of tautology.

(Don't just take my word for it. The esteemed Lake District poet Norman Nicholson (1914-1987) confronted the issue long before I did, although it seems he was rather more forgiving. 'A certain excuse for the tautology can be made in the case of Windermere, since we need to differentiate between the lake and the town,' he said, 'though it would be better to speak of "Windermere Lake" and "Windermere Town", but no one can excuse such ridiculous clumsiness as "Lake Derwentwater" and "Lake Ullswater".')

So Bassenthwaite is indeed a lake.

And of all the bigger Lake District lakes it was the one I knew least well.

And so it would doubtless have remained had I not been planning my next Bongo Night – S in my Lake District A-Z – at the time I spotted that Val McDermid was one of the celebrity speakers appearing at Words by the Water, a book festival held every year at the Theatre by the Lake in Keswick.

Not that I knew very much about her.

I had not read any of her books – indeed I'm not sure I even knew she had written any – but I had long ago been captivated by the common sense she spoke in her regular slots in 'A Point of View', the Radio 4 programme that slowly drags me out of a sleepy unconsciousness every Sunday morning.

I knew that she spoke great wisdom in a soft and enchanting Scottish accent, and that was enough. As soon as I heard she was appearing in Keswick, I bought myself a ticket . . . and then set out to make everything else fit around it.

She has sold so many books (16 million at the last count) and won so many prizes that she probably would not include in her list of achievements in the world of literature the fact that she played a part in my Bongo Nights tour of the Lake District.

Yet it was my pursuit of this so-called 'Queen of Crime' – as a staunch republican she hates the title, apparently – that took me to a little place called Scarness, tucked away largely undiscovered on the eastern shore of Bassenthwaite Lake.

If I could find somewhere near Keswick whose name began with S, I had thought, I would be able to satisfy myself twice over by combining McDermid's visit with the next stop on my A-Z Bongo Nights tour.

And so . . . to Scarness, a tiny community just five miles from Keswick, overlooking the lake, but tucked away where few people bother to venture, and therefore a perfect spot for me to spend a night.

Scarness is, in reality, not much of a community at all – just an early 18th century cottage important enough to be a listed building, a scattering of other houses and the Bassenthwaite Lakeside Lodges holiday park where, if you happen to have £100,000 or so burning holes in your pockets, you can buy one of 56 chalets in which, the developers will tell you, you can spend your holidays enjoying 'breathtaking views, tranquil surroundings and wonderful walks' in 'the shelter of the dramatic Skiddaw mountain range'.

In truth, if you're the sort of person who likes that sort of thing, you could do a lot worse when choosing a holiday destination. The scenery is indeed breathtaking, and the chalets – sorry, 'lodges' – seem to be several notches superior to most others I have seen.

I am, though, not that sort of person, and for me Scarness was just a place in which, for just one night, I would be happy to park my Bongo while briefly enjoying the company of Val McDermid.

It's true that it boasts no parking places with wonderful views of either lake or mountains – the holiday park lodges have bagged all of those – but there are plenty of spots to park safely, and on level ground well off the road, which are handy for some easy and idyllic country walks by day and promise to be quiet and undisturbed by night.

I parked on a muddy verge a quarter of a mile down the road from the houses, just a few paces from where a signpost directed me diagonally across open countryside in the direction of the main reason I was there – a tiny church standing all alone in the middle of a field.

If you chanced upon St Bega's in a town, or even in an olde worlde chocolate-box village, you probably would not give it a second glance, but standing there on the banks of the lake, in the shadow of a 3,000ft mountain, it looks like the most enchanting place you could ever wish to see.

The church is reckoned to date from before 1000 AD and is one of only three (all of them in Cumbria) dedicated to Saint Bega, who, according to legend, was a princess who in the seventh century fled to England to escape from the Viking chieftain she was supposed to be marrying in Ireland.

She landed at St Bees, just south of Whitehaven, and for years lived in poverty and (more important to her) chastity in what is now Cumbria until she became so scared of the pirates who raided the coast in those days that she moved east to continue her life of piety in Northumberland.

Not surprisingly the church and the area around it has become a favourite among poets and writers over the years – not least William Wordsworth, who wrote of it in his 'Guide to the English Lakes', and Alfred, Lord Tennyson, who is reputed to have been inspired to describe it ('a chapel nigh the field, a broken chancel with a broken cross, that stood on a dark straight of barren land') in the opening lines of 'Morte d'Arthur'.

More recently Melvyn Bragg – or, more accurately Lord Bragg of Wigton, after the Cumbrian town in which he grew up – has joined the list of artistic folk who have found something very special there.

A small framed notice in the church includes these words from the man who has become the television age's guide to all things intellectual:

'When I was at school I used to cycle with friends into the Lake District, usually to the most northerly of the Lakes – Bassenthwaite. There we would hire a boat and row across to a small, dramatically isolated church on the edge of the lake . . .

'It has become one of my favourite haunts in the whole of the Lake District. Even today it is not at all difficult to spend hours around and about the church in virtual isolation.'

Little surprise, then, that in his book 'Credo' Bragg chose to write a fictionalised account of St Bega's life . . . or that in 2019, shortly before his 80th birthday, he chose to get married there.

The church – one of those happy establishments which is left open every day – is still regularly used as a place of worship and boasts that it houses Bibles in 30 languages so that the visitors who flock to it from all over the world feel at home.

What it no longer has (which was a disappointment to me, since I had been looking forward to seeing it) was the unusual egg-timer-like hour-glass which used to tell preachers when their sermons had gone on too long.

These days the glass is gone, and all there is to see, still attached to the pillar closest to the pulpit, is the ancient wrought-iron bracket in which it used to sit.

I had had enough of trying to find a firm path through the soggy field on my way to the church, so my plan as I left was to walk a little way back along the road before taking a footpath to the left, which would lead me on a scenic route alongside the lake all the way back to Scarness. But that idea evaporated once I paused to chat with a charming old lady – a local, even though her heavy rucsac gave her the look of a visiting Wainwright-bagger – I met at the gate out of the churchyard.

I told her where I was heading and she grimaced.

'That looks good on the map,' she agreed, 'but it's probably not so good in real life. It should be a lovely walk but I'm afraid it's not. It's always muddy, even in high summer, and after the rain we had last week it will be impassable.'

'That's OK,' I told her. 'I have a plan B.'

I did not like to admit that my alternative plan was just a lazier version of plan A.

It would involve walking the short distance back to the Bongo and driving, not walking, back to Scarness village before taking a footpath from there down to the lake, and I would do it for no better reason than I did not want to go home without seeing Bassenthwaite from an angle I had never seen before.

The path I found was one that skirted the holiday park – deserted apart from a hardy couple dressed from head to toe in all-weather gear as they struggled to overcome some problem beneath their chalet – and ended on a series of slippery stepping stones and wooden walkways leading, it seemed, directly into the lake.

This, I realised, must be the other end of the 'impassable' path that the friendly lady at the church had warned me not to take and it was only a sudden hail shower that persuaded me not to follow it.

I dashed back to the Bongo, my mission accomplished.

Bassenthwaite, my unknown lake, was a mystery no more. I had seen it from every angle, walked beside it, investigated a little of its history and experienced the best and the worst of its weather.

And still I had an hour or so with Val McDermid to look forward to, followed by fish and chips from the Old Keswickian in the Square, all of which, I knew, would set me up nicely for a return to my parking place in the mud at Scarness, and a happy hour watching 'Rumpole of the Bailey' before bedtime. S for Scarness. S for serendipity.

The Theatre by the Lake, as its name implies, is a mere stone's throw from Derwentwater, so any visit to it – whether for a talk, a show or just a coffee in its airy cafe – is enhanced by a stroll to the lakeside before or after, or both.

It was there, as I leaned on a wall enjoying the view down to Castle Crag, which was rather surprisingly bathed in evening sunshine at the far end of the lake, that I had time to ponder the metaphorical dark cloud that was looming in the distance.

The radio news that day had been dominated by worries of some kind of flu which, it seemed, had begun in China and had already spread to many parts of mainland Europe.

That day a couple of cases had been reported in the North East of England and we were being warned to take a few simple precautions now to prevent it spreading any further.

This coronavirus, as they called it, seemed to be a pretty distant thing, though virulent in the places in which it had taken hold, so the advice amounted to little more than to avoid anyone who had a cough or a sneeze.

When I returned to the theatre I discovered that I had fortuitously booked myself into a part of the auditorium apparently not favoured by many others, so I was able to settle down in my seat with nobody else – coughing or not – within several feet of me.

It was a happy way to spend an evening (Val McDermid is a wonderfully entertaining raconteur) and I returned to Scarness contemplating yet again how my nights in the Bongo had a habit of introducing me to places and people I would never have otherwise have encountered.

I settled down in a small layby beside a gate, just down the road from where I had parked in the afternoon, and neither saw nor heard another human being until well past breakfast time next morning.

If I had known that it would be my last Bongo Night for many months I would have appreciated it even more.

20
Tarn Moor

Over the next couple of weeks the advice became rather more than just to avoid people with coughs and sneezes.

The coronavirus outbreak – or pandemic as it was increasingly being called – was taking hold in this country as well as in most others around the world, and it was clearly only a matter of time before we would be ordered not to leave our homes.

It was Tricia's birthday, though, and, we guessed, our last opportunity to get out into the Lake District before the lockdown that we knew was coming would put us under house arrest for who knew how long (in fact we chose to begin our self isolation the very next day – a few days before the government told us we had to, just as we finished it several days after it told us we could).

Even at that early stage of the crisis the news of the rapidly spreading virus was enough to deter us from going to any of the Lake District's tourist honeypot places, not just because it had become very obvious that crowds were best avoided but also because the locals living in such places were anxiously trying to keep visitors at bay so as to prevent the disease spreading there.

So we headed for a place we were confident most people did not know about – an expanse of wild moorland so huge that the few people likely to be there would not need to come within several hundred metres of each other.

This place was Tarn Moor, one of my favourite undiscovered places in Cumbria.

It lies to the east of Ullswater, almost as close to the Pennines as it is to the mountains of the Lake District and is reached by roads that seem at first to be winding their way away from their destination rather than towards it.

Once you are there, alone (or almost alone) in that mind boggling sweep of open countryside, you are rewarded with what is, in my judgment anyway, one of the finest views in England, as Ullswater almost magically comes into view – seeming to rise out of the ground with each step that you take, like the organs that used to rise from beneath the floor in the black and white days of the early cinema.

Not that you can park a Bongo or any other vehicle at that precise point, of course.

The spot where the view of Ullswater suddenly unfolds below you is happily distant from anywhere that can be negotiated by anything less robust than a farmer's quadbike. But it is possible to get quite close.

You can park your car – or, if you are lucky, your Bongo – beside the road, then set off on foot, heading west on a gentle track across the moor, and as you do so some of Lakeland's most impressive fells begin to appear in front of you – Helvellyn and Blencathra – before Ullswater comes into view.

I have said before that Ullswater is my favourite lake, and the sight of it from those fells – so close, yet so wonderfully undiscovered by almost every tourist – never fails to take my breath away and to tickle my eyes with tears.

I include it here, in this A-Z book of Lake District Bongo Nights, not because on that occasion – just hours before the whole country went into lockdown, I was planning to sleep there, but because it is one of my favourite places in the whole of the Lake District.

It was the last place Tricia and I went to before we were banned from going anywhere at all, and – as I shall explain – the first place we went to afterwards.

And, since it is a place in which I did indeed spend a Bongo Night some years before, I feel entitled to include it here.

My night on Tarn Moor, back when I was writing my first Bongo Nights book, came about because, quite frankly I was too tired to go anywhere else.

I knew that a few hours in the Bongo, in a place I loved so much and which just happened to be less than an hour from my home, would be all the recharging my batteries would need, both physically and mentally.

I set off south down the M6, armed with little more than a flask of tea, two Tupperware boxes (one containing a salad for my supper, and the other bacon, eggs and mushrooms for my breakfast) and an old tracksuit to sleep in.

I turned off the motorway at Penrith, and initially followed the signs to Haweswater before diving to the right, up an unlikely-looking lane that shoots sharply past the last few houses and onto the fellside. Within a mile all sign of civilisation has gone and, were it not for the narrow ribbon of tarmac winding through the gorse, you might think nobody had ever been there before.

They have, of course. It's a favourite place for dog walkers, and for fell walkers who don't mind cheating by using a car to gain them the first thousand feet before they set off on foot to conquer some peak or other, but on that night the only sign of human life was a single car parked in a rough lay-by, pointing towards the Pennines to the east, which were already turning gold under the setting sun.

I drove on till I could no longer see it and pulled onto the flattest patch of grass I could find.

Behind me the sun was falling towards the horizon of the moorland, in front of me the hills were spread out in a glorious panorama that dimmed even as I watched it, and to my left an extraordinary brown cloud blotted out any hope of a view, a sure sign that Penrith and all the other places I had passed through to get there were now being drenched in a sudden squall.

The only sound I could hear was of the wind gently whistling over the Bongo.

The peacefulness, the aloneness, was something to savour.

Then three young men, none of whom looked old enough to drive, arrived in a small convoy, and parked their cars side by side, in a neat row not more than 20 feet from me.

Their cars – all shining and beautifully polished, with the very latest accessories gleaming in the dying light – were clearly their pride and joy.

They took photographs of them against the setting sun (but only after using their sleeves to wipe off any suggestion of dirt they had picked up on their drive into the hills) and then manoeuvred them a few yards so they could take some more with the sun at a better angle.

In other circumstances – faced with three teenagers on some lonely and increasingly dark hillside – I might have been troubled by a certain apprehension.

But, though I longed for them to go away and leave me to myself, this was the least threatening trio I could have hoped to encounter.

Soon enough they drove off as suddenly as they had arrived and I watched in surprise as they took a course not along the road, but over the rough moorland, dodging the bumps and hollows as if they were chasing wildebeest on some overland safari.

I was still trying to work out how they could dish out such treatment to the cars they obviously loved so much when their tail lights disappeared from view behind the undergrowth. I have no idea whether they continued their journey home on some rough track, or doubled back to the road so they could do it on the more welcoming tarmac, but they were gone and that was all that mattered.

I didn't see another soul until I was cooking breakfast the next morning. And by that time I had already been for a walk over the fell to the place where I could enjoy that view, down over Ullswater.

It was a perfect morning for it. So perfect that I was already walking by six o'clock. The early sun was shining brightly, the sky was blue and the lake, when it came into view, was a deep purple.

I sat on a rock, with the skylarks singing their beautiful songs just for me.

Five years later and the skylarks were still singing when Tricia and I were there on lockdown eve.

A few other people had had the same idea – spending a day in a beautiful place while we still could, before we were all confined to our homes for who knew how long.

The sun was shining, the sky was blue and the breeze was gentle and warm . . . and everything was right with the world apart from the deadly plague that was sweeping in from the east to change our lives for ever.

There was a certain melancholy in the air, and a feeling of uncertainty, and the way we gave a wide berth to the few people we met was strangely unsettling even if we had no idea that this was how we would be living our lives for very many months to come.

We spent only a couple of hours tramping across the moor, pausing for a picnic in the remains of an ancient stone circle and – of course – reaching the place where the view of Ullswater rises up in the near distance.

It was a day it seemed important to savour especially deeply, to enjoy the views and rejoice in the singing of the skylarks more than ever before. Or, for all we knew, more than ever again.

It was three months before we were allowed out of our homes to go once again to the Lake District – three months in which the headlines had been full not just of the pandemic's mounting death toll, and the debate over the government's response to it, but on a more local level of worries about the dangers of unwelcome tourists spreading the virus into Lake District communities singularly ill equipped to deal with it.

A few people – too ignorant or too selfish to believe that the pleas to stay away included even them – had continued to visit the National Park, causing great levels of both anger and fear.

But most of us stayed away, accepting the need to protect the Lake District and its inhabitants, even though one of the things we longed for above all else was the chance to walk once again across its wild open fells.

When the opportunity to do that again came it felt . . . well, strange.

But when the total lockdown was eased, and people were allowed to use their cars for something more than just 'essential' travel, and when Lake District communities came to accept it – probably grudgingly, and certainly fearfully – Tricia and I decided to have another picnic on Tarn Moor.

There seemed no more appropriate place to resume our love affair with our home county.

When we got there the skylarks were singing more loudly and, it seemed, more joyously than ever.

I truly had never heard such a sound. And probably for the first time in my life I understood what people meant when they said the air was full of birdsong. Their singing was loud and incessant and it really did fill the air.

The sky was blue, with just a few fluffy white clouds building up over the Pennines behind us in the west, and we set off across the fells with happy hearts.

We did not intent to go very far – our weeks of lockdown had got us out of the habit of long walks – but we reckoned we would probably make it far enough to catch our first glimpse of Ullswater for three months.

We stopped for a picnic on the rocky remains of what we took to be some sort of neolithic building, and I took the opportunity to enjoy my new-found freedom by stretching out on the blanket in the sun.

There was no escaping the fact that the few white fluffy clouds were becoming altogether darker and more threatening, though.

And the rumbling sound of thunder in the distance confirmed that the weather was changing.

Fast.

We gathered up our stuff and looked at our intended viewpoint on the horizon, working out that we just about had enough time to reach it before the weather would force us to turn back.

We didn't get that far though. We were less than half way there when we reluctantly accepted that the weather had broken much more quickly than we had expected – a few spots of rain were beginning to fall, the occasional rumble had become a constant roar as the thunderstorm engulfed the next valley, and the flashes of lightning were now much closer and more frightening.

Tricia and I – separately, and yet together – decided enough was enough.

How hideously ironic it would be, we thought, if after going to such lengths to avoid succumbing to the coronavirus we should meet our ends by being struck by lightning on a remote Cumbrian moor.

By the time we got back within sight of the car the sky was black and it was raining steadily.

By the time we were sitting inside it we were soaked to the skin and the lightning was crashing right above our heads.

It was raining like I had not seen it rain for years.

But who cared? We were back in the Lake District. And, with any luck, I would soon be back in the Bongo, spending the night in some place beginning with U.

It was then that the whole idea of my Bongo Nights became illegal not just in theory, but in practice too.

It was Covid19 that was to blame.

To celebrate their new-found freedom after months of being locked down in their homes, campervanners in their hundreds headed immediately to the one place they knew that could be relied upon to repair their broken spirits: The Lake District.

They began to take over, it seemed, every wildcamping space for miles around – beside lakes, by rivers, on top of hills, on farm verges and on every patch of accessible land they could find.

Not surprisingly the police, in association with the Lake District National Park Authority, decided that, for the good of the very landscape that these people had come to enjoy, something had to be done.

They invoked the long-ignored bye-law – 'no one shall camp in tent or van' etc - and started moving people on.

Disgruntled campers complained that the police had come knocking on their doors in the middle of the night to tell them that if they wanted to sleep in their vans they would have to do it outside the boundaries of the National Park.

At first I was disgruntled too – not least because it threw into question the whole ethos of my Bongo Nights A-Z challenge just when I was within sight of completing it.

But a moment's more thought told me they were quite right.

The Lake District cannot sustain such numbers, and even though, I like to think, I had enough local knowledge to find places that others would not find, and I always made a point of parking well away from any houses or other campervans and usually ended up bringing home more litter than I took, I reluctantly had to concede that there couldn't be one set of rules for me and one for everyone else.

If it was in the Lake District's interests to ban wildcamping – albeit, I hoped, temporarily – it had to include me.

My problem then was how I could continue my A-Z adventure without falling foul of the new rules.

I could, of course, have just carried on, spending my nights in places so remote that no officer of the law was likely to find me, or I could have put the whole thing on hold, and waited until winter when (I presumed) the police would have found something else to do with their time.

But both those solutions – and a host of others – smacked too much of breaking the rules, or at least bending them, and that was something I was reluctant to do for fear of suggesting that I, because I was lucky enough to be local, did not have to protect the environment that I loved quite as fiercely as other people who weren't.

The solution, when it came to me, was simple: I would continue my mission by doing Bongo Nights in exactly the same way as the real thing . . . except that I would not actually go to sleep.

I would arrive at my chosen spot early in the morning, at the time I would normally be waking up there, I would cook my breakfast, I would explore the area, go for a walk, read a book, listen to the radio, play my guitar and do all the other things I would do on a traditional Bongo Night . . . and then, when it was time to go to bed, I would drive home.

It seemed the most appropriate way of keeping the spirit of Bongo Nights alive while also accepting that the Lake District had a right to protect itself – even if it was protecting itself against people like me.

21
Uldale

I was up to U in my A-Z, which meant my chosen spot was only half an hour from home.

Uldale is a small village tucked away in the northern fells, half way up the hill that leads to the glorious expanse of wildness that surrounds the bigger and better known village of Caldbeck.

It has a range of small mountains named after it – the Uldale Fells include such walkers' delights as Longlands, Knott and the schoolboys' favourite, Great Cockup – and, to the north and east of it, it gives its name to Uldale Common, a 4,000 hectare wonderland of what is now wild open countryside but was once an industrial landscape of mines and quarry workings.

It is crisscrossed by numerous enticing paths on which it is possible to spend a whole day just wandering, enjoying the views, listening to the singing of the birds and wallowing in the carpet of wildflowers under your feet.

And it was beside one of those paths, in a rough parking space well off the road and big enough for two or three cars, that I arrived early, to cook my breakfast.

I had arranged to meet my friends Pat and Eddie Stephenson, who had been with me when I had visited Eycott Hill early on in my A-Z travels.

I had invited them to be my guides because they lived just a few miles away, over the hill from Uldale, and knew these parts much better than I.

We headed north along the path and after just a few minutes breasted the small hill and found ourselves looking down on an area which, even to my inexpert eye, betrayed the signs of earlier human habitation.

'Aughertree ancient village,' said Eddie, pronouncing the name 'Affa-tree', and declaring it to be the remains of a Bronze Age village.

Pat and Eddie had seen the settlement from afar on numerous occasions, but never before had they had the time to get any closer.

'Let's go down and take a look,' I said.

The trouble with such sites is that they are best seen from above (Eddie's best views came years ago when he was flying a glider over it) and by the time we had walked down to investigate it the clear shape of the earthworks had morphed into a vague collection of lumps and bumps which really made no sense at all.

It was the OS app on our mobiles that helped us. Technology is so sophisticated these days that our phones were able to pinpoint our location within, it seemed a few inches, so we were able to position ourselves precisely in the right place.

We walked – or, in my case, stumbled, because I have a talent for falling over any unseen holes and tussocks – across the fell until the red arrows signifying our location were precisely in the middle of the circles portraying the ancient buildings on the map on our mobiles.

And sure enough we could now see that the vague lumps and bumps could indeed have represented the outline of some ancient community.

'There is supposed to be a stone circle somewhere here too,' I said, encouraged by our success at locating the village.

But finding the stone circle was even more difficult than finding the village – not least because we could not rely on technology to help us.

Perhaps it is because we were secretly expecting something that looked like Stonehenge – or the impressive monument at Castlerigg just 12 miles down the road – but there was nothing that looked like what we were looking for.

We knew the approximate map reference and we all walked in different directions where it should have been. Eddie walked this way, Pat walked that, and I walked somewhere in between, but none of us could find anything that could have been a neolithic stone circle.

Just a few random stones, most almost buried in the soft ground, dotted around the landscape like dice thrown by an angry giant.

'It's right under our feet,' Eddie said at last. 'Just look.'

And he was right of course, the random stones did indeed form a circle – about 50 metres diameter – and just because they weren't standing up and attracting tourists in their thousands did not make them any less special.

Indeed, the fact that we had found them on a remote hillside somehow made them more so.

Our mission accomplished, we continued along the route I had drawn up in my head.

A diversion here to see the remains of an impressive lime kiln, a pause there to see a beautiful stained glass window in a renovated farmhouse, and a linger in the road outside a house that would have been flattened if a huge oak tree, now no more than a stump, had fallen onto it rather than away from it in the storms . . .

It was a walk filled with just as much interest as I had hoped when I had seen it on the map. The route from the village of Aughertree (a quiet and tiny place now, but once a bustling village with several taverns to satisfy the needs of the workers from its many farms and quarries) took us down a narrow farm track which became even narrower and more enclosed by hedges as it headed in a straight line towards a little white church peeping out from between the trees a mile or so away.

This was the funeral road, the route that the people of Aughertree would once have walked, carrying the coffins of their loved ones to Uldale's 'old church'.

The church, dedicated to St James, dates back to about 1150, though you wouldn't guess it since so much of it was rebuilt in the 18th century.

It is a lovely, simple little place, perfectly fitting the solitude of its surroundings, but after arriving at it via the funeral road it was the tombstones in the graveyard that surrounds it that I found most evocative.

It was easy to imagine the tearful little corteges making their way there across the fields from the village, easy to see the sturdy farmhands all dressed in black, with the coffins on their shoulders, and easy to feel their pain as they said goodbye to those they had loved.

One stone in particular brought a picture that was especially vivid – that of a small child.

Her coffin would have been tiny, and I imagined her father carrying her in his arms every inch of the way, with her mother following behind in tears.

Another tombstone – just about the biggest in the graveyard – commemorated the passing of one Thomas Tomlinson, an 'able and satisfactory' teacher at the local school, whose memorial was erected by three of his old pupils.

I could not help but wonder how happy a schoolmaster would be to be described, after a lifetime of teaching, as no more than 'satisfactory' . . . or, after having had in his hands the learning of perhaps hundreds of local children, only three of them had bothered to club together to erect a tombstone in his honour.

From the church my route took us the mile along a quiet country road to the village of Uldale, where the old village school – opened in 1895 and closed in the 1990s – is now an excellent tea shop and art gallery.

Half an hour later I was back at the Bongo and ready for a burger.

I lifted the elevating roof to give myself more room, moved my guitar out of the way onto the passenger seat, found the frying pan, lit the gas and settled down into as close as I was going to get to a proper Bongo Night meal.

Except it was not a Bongo Night, of course.

And before long I realised I had better start making plans to go home before some passing policeman – or a policeman alerted by some local farmer, who I had heard, was happy to act as the eyes and ears of the custodians of the law, especially when it came to reporting on campervans disregarding the new restrictions – happened to come by.

I started the engine, pressed the switch to lower the roof . . . and nothing happened.

Now this was something I had often worried about: What do you do if you are in some remote spot, many miles away from help, and find that for some reason the roof gets stuck in the 'up' position?

There is, as far as I know, no way of bringing the roof down manually, so if the electrical system chooses not to work you are . . . well, stuck.

For a moment, confess, I panicked.

But then I saw the funny side. There I was trapped, with dusk fast approaching, in a place where campervans were not allowed to spend the night, but in a campervan which could not be moved.

What, I wondered, would that passing policeman make of it?

'I'm sorry, sir. You will have to go home. You are not allowed to camp here.'

'I'm sorry too, officer. I want to go home as much as you want me to. But I have no choice. I can't drive with the roof up, and I can't get it down.'

I was almost looking forward to my encounter with The Law, whose representative, I was confident, would have no better solution than I had myself.

But then common sense took over and I phoned the AA, but doubting whether their mechanic would know what to do either I adopted the belt-and-braces technique of posting a message on the Facebook pages of two Bongo owners' groups.

'Help!' I wrote. 'I'm stuck in the middle of nowhere and my roof won't come down. Any suggestions?'

To my surprise, the replies started coming in almost immediately, and though most of them were of no assistance at all one of them did look promising.

'This happened to me,' said one helpful chap. 'I didn't have a clue what to do so I just drove a few yards with the roof still up, then tried again and – bingo! – it came down easy as anything.'

Having nothing to lose (except a potentially enjoyable encounter with a policeman) I followed his advice.

I started the engine, drove forwards no more than ten feet, reached up to the switch that controls the roof and – just as the man said – bingo!

The roof came down just as smoothly as it was supposed to.

The AA operator sensed a hint of disappointment in my voice when I rang her to call off the mechanic.

'That's really good news,' she said, doubtfully.

I didn't like to tell her why I was disappointed.

What it meant, though, was that I now had so little confidence in the Bongo's elevating roof I would never risk raising it again for fear that it would not close when I needed it to.

Only one man could help – Tim Wing at the Bongo Barn.

It was, he told me with a polite smile, a common problem, especially for Bongos whose electrically operated hydraulic roof-lifting system is not regularly serviced.

I did not dare to tell him – but I suspect he knew it anyway – that in all the eight years I had owned the Bongo I had never had the roof mechanism serviced at all.

It took him only a couple of hours to fix it – time enough for me to inspect a small fleet of Bongos he had just shipped in from Japan.

Importing Bongos (he has a team of helpers in Japan, scouring the country for good secondhand examples), restoring them to tip-top condition and selling them on to an increasingly eager market in Britain is what Tim does alongside his garage business.

It's a thriving business, because despite its age (production ceased in 2005 when the factory burned down) the Bongo is becoming an increasingly popular alternative to the bigger, more luxurious but far less versatile motorhomes that we see lording it down our motorways every bank holiday weekend.

Bongos have a special place in the world of motor vehicles because for a long time they were the only ones actually designed and built right from the start as campervans.

Everything else – apart from a few top-of-the-range monsters that cost as much as a small house – was designed as a van and modified later.

'They were originally intended for travelling salesmen and sales reps in Japan – people who wanted something they could sleep in, eat in, do their office work in and drive,' Tim told me over a cup of tea in his workshop.

'They're like a mobile Travel Lodge. There's never been anything like them.'

Most Bongos come to this country in their original state – eight-seater people carriers, with two seats in the front and two bench seats in the back that can be folded down to make a full-sized bed – but once here they can, if necessary, be adapted in a host of ways.

Some, like mine, are given the full works, with pull-out bed, cupboards, sink, fridge, gas hob and electricity supply; some are fitted with a mini kitchen that can be installed or extracted within minutes; and some can have any variation in between.

'I spend a lot of time finding out what people want, what sort of lives they live and what they want to use them for,' Tim said, as if he was talking about helping a man find his dream date. 'That way I can make sure they get the Bongo that will suit them.'

I dragged myself away from the attractive idea of buying myself a new Bongo and returned to the one I already had.

'It's all fixed – give it a try,' said Tim.

I pushed the switch and the roof opened smoothly, effortlessly and with little more than a whisper – a far cry from the creaking and groaning I had become used to.

'I've fixed the fuel gauge too,' he said.

'That hasn't worked for about five years,' I confessed.

'And I've taken a look underneath. I'm afraid it needs a bit of work.'

Now, I'm at heart, a suspicious type, certainly not gullible enough to fall for every trick a dodgy garage man might try to get more work, and therefore more money, out of me. But Tim is someone I trust. He exudes honesty and trustfulness and if he was telling me the Bongo required a major overhaul I was not going to doubt him.

'OK just tell me what needs doing,' I told him. 'I'm relying on you to keep it going. I haven't finished the alphabet yet.'

22

Vale of Lorton

Lorton, the village at the head of the vale that takes its name, is a smashing little place – a pretty community in a wonderful location but with none of the down sides (too many people, too much traffic and too much reliance on shops selling tacky souvenirs) that besmirch so many other pretty places in wonderful locations.

It's well away from most of the area's honeypots, on the north-western fringe of the national park, and closer to the industrial bleakness of places like Workington than it is to the tourist-hungry enclaves of Ambleside and Grasmere, and the best way of getting to it is through what feels like the Lake District's back door.

It's true that the road over Whinlatter – the Mecca for anyone with a mountain bike, thanks to the exciting trails that criss-cross the steep Forestry Commission land at the top – can be quite busy, but once you start the descent from there you enter a world that feels far removed from mass tourism.

Lorton itself – strictly speaking it is two villages, Low Lorton and High Lorton, though it is hard to tell where one ends and the other begins – lies at the bottom of the hill, at the northern end of the Vale through which flows the River Cocker.

On the way I took a short diversion, venturing right when I could have gone left, just to visit what must be Britain's smallest national nature reserve.

Sandybeck Meadow, tucked in beside a narrow country lane and the picturesque bridge it goes over, looks nothing very special at all and is so small (less than half a hectare) you can just look over the wall and see the whole of it.

The meadow has never in living memory been ploughed and to this day is managed using only traditional farming methods, with the hay never being cut until after the flowering season is over.

As a result it supports a rich diversity of plant species, including some that are scarce nationally, and at the right time of year it becomes a magical paintbox of wild flowers the like of which exists nowhere else.

It would be easy to miss it altogether were it not for the small Natural England notice.

'Sandybeck Meadow represents a rare and important remnant of traditionally managed hay meadow, most of which have been lost through agricultural improvement,' it says.

'The delights of this meadow appear when the first spring flowers such as wood anemone and common bistort begin to show. But it's in late June through to mid August when the meadow bursts into full flower with beauties such as greater butterfly orchid, great burnet and betony.'

From there it was only a couple of miles to the lay-by, just south of Lorton, where I parked.

It was a large flat gravel area and it would, I am certain, have afforded me with a peaceful place to sleep had it been a lawful option.

As it was, it was still early enough for me to cook breakfast before leaving the Bongo there and walking back to see whatever sights the village had to offer.

A good place to start in any community is the local noticeboard, and reading them is something I have done assiduously for more than 50 years, ever since I was a fledgling newspaper reporter and my first editor sent me out to in the villages that made up my patch with the instruction to 'find some news'.

I quickly discovered that most village noticeboards were a rich source of the sort of news stories that made newspapers like the Weston-super-Mare Mercury worth reading – appeals for help to mend the church roof, news of the local school's sponsored walk, small notices announcing the end of a 60-year career spent teaching the locality's children to play the piano, old ladies thanking mystery strangers for picking up their shopping after their accident . . . if you looked hard enough you would find it.

I was pleased to see that the Low Lorton noticeboard continued this tradition.

A notice from the Friends of the Lake District exhorting residents to turn off their lights as part of a Dark Skies campaign, a warning that the village seemed to have been struck by an unpleasant-sounding disease that threatened the lives of its garden birds (they 'look lethargic, sleepy, fluffed up, have difficulty breathing and are reluctant to fly') and an invitation to visitors to spend some time in the nearby community garden, which had been 'newly renovated' into a place where 'everyone can enjoy the plants and the view over the stream'.

The garden was through a small gate next to the village hall – for many years a brewery, until in 1910 its owners, the Jennings Brothers, moved to a bigger, more advanced place in Cockermouth, a few miles up the road – and it was a real joy.

A single bench, set among lovely blue agapanthus, white phlox and purple bears' breeches, and all overlooking the tumbling waters of the Whit Beck as it made its way towards the Cocker. It was a simple oasis of peace in a place which was already so peaceful it really had no need of one.

I wondered how many people were too busy ever to have found it.

On the far side of the stream was Low Lorton's only claim to fame – a huge yew tree, thought to be more than 1,000 years old.

At its peak, in the early 1800s, its girth was measured as 24ft, but soon after that it broke in two, leaving it much reduced – with wood from the broken half being taken to make a chair for the mayor of Cockermouth.

The tree has some religious significance too. John Wesley, founder of Methodism, preached under it several times in the 1750s, and

George Fox, founder of the Quakers, did the same 'to a large crowd that included soldiers from Cromwell's army'.

And of course, this being the Lake District, William Wordsworth got in on the act too . . . His poem 'Yew Trees' begins 'There is a yew tree, pride of Lorton Vale' and talks of its timbers being used for the bows used at the battle of Agincourt.

From Lorton the view down the valley is dominated by the mighty Grasmoor fell on the left, with the lesser shapes of Red Pike, Starling Dodd and Melbreak, almost beckoning us to go from this quiet and unknown place to explore deeper into the heart of the Lake District which lies so tantalisingly close.

I had neither the time nor the inclination to climb any mountains, but I did want to explore the bottom end of the Vale, where a path through a wood would lead me to the northern tip of Crummock Water, from where, I knew, there was one of the best views in the Lake District.

I could have walked but instead I went back to the Bongo and drove the three miles to a National Trust car park tucked away in the trees beside a road bridge over the River Cocker.

From there a rough path (very rough in places, after recent rain that had washed much of it away) led upstream on the banks of the Cocker, over a sluice gate and a weir, to the spot where it suddenly emerges from the trees into the glorious expanse of the lake stretching the two-and-a-half miles down towards Buttermere.

I am no expert in the Lake District mountains (either climbing them or being able to recognise them) but I can tell you that from that spot the lovely lake of Crummock is surrounded by some of the finest of them. Red Pike, High Stile, Great Gable, Scafell Pike, Haystacks, Helvellyn, Grisedale Pike . . . all these (and I can only tell you by looking at the map) are spread out in a great arc in the sort of panorama that you see in those huge arty photographs that you find in the windows of upmarket souvenir shops.

I stood there on a pebbly beach, absorbing the view, knowing that no photograph could ever do it justice.

23
Waterside

There came a time when, after so long exploring all that's most beautiful in the most beautiful part of the country, I started hankering for something just a bit different.

Something maybe just a little less perfect.

Just as when I came home desperate for egg and beans on toast after a fortnight of eating the finest food on a Mediterranean cruise (I got sent on one for free, courtesy of the newspaper I was working for at the time), I found I wanted something, dare I say, a little grittier and more like real life.

In Cumbria, you can't get much grittier than Cleator Moor – a small town in which all the imperfections and harshness of modern life is on open, often desperate, display.

It is a town I have always had a sneaking respect for – perhaps because it so often finds itself condemned by people who, I suspect, have never been there.

The moment I first arrived in Cumbria more than 30 years ago, I noticed that Cleator Moor was a place usually spoken about in hushed tones, with the speaker adopting the gloomy tone of voice more appropriate to some dreadful unhappiness or disease before embarking on a damning catalogue of crime, violence and unemployment,

It is a town with problems, true enough; but it's a town with a history that makes it one of the most interesting in the county, and when I discovered that just down the road was a place called Waterside – less a place than a couple of farms and a cottage, if I'm honest – I knew it was there that I had to go to for my 23rd Bongo Night.

While the town is just outside the Lake District National Park, Waterside is just inside, so I could satisfy my self imposed criteria – all these Bongo Nights had to be spent with the Bongo parked inside the Lake District – by parking in a small lay-by at Waterside and then walking along the road beside the river until I reached Cleator Moor.

The water that I parked beside – and the water that gives Waterside its name – is the Ehen, a pretty, tumbling little river that meanders its way from Ennerdale on the west of the Lake District to the Irish Sea, which it enters just north of the blot on the landscape that is the Sellafield nuclear reprocessing site.

I parked the Bongo with its bonnet facing the incredible panorama over Ennerdale and towards the western fells.

And then I turned my back on the Lake District and walked the other way.

It was a disappointment that I could not immediately dangle my toes at least metaphorically in the river – an extraordinary amount of barbed wire saw to that – but within half a mile or so I got my reward.

Wath Bridge is a delightful spot – a big grassy patch with benches and picnic tables right beside the river, with space for half a dozen cars to be parked without any risk of blocking the road or having to pay for the privilege.

It would have been an ideal Bongo Nights spot . . . if it had not been a yard or two outside the National Park.

Cleator Moor, let's be clear, is not an especially pretty town.

In fact parts of it – not least the huge housing estate that makes up half of the town – are downright ugly,

But as I began my five-mile ramble around its streets and footpaths I realised the ugliest thing of all is its poverty.

Cleator Moor was little more than a wild stretch of moorland until, in the 1870s, huge amounts of iron ore and, to a lesser extent, coal were discovered just below the surface.

Iron ore had been mined in the area in a small way for generations – it is known that monks in nearby Egremont had their own workings as early as the 12th century – but it was only in the mid 19th century that it hit the big time.

Suddenly this sleepy and long ignored part of Cumbria became the centre of an industrial upheaval not unlike the Klondike gold rush of the Yukon a few decades later.

The more iron was demanded by the Industrial Revolution, the more Cleator Moor obliged, with mines being built all across the area, and a crisscross maze of railway lines being constructed to transport the stuff down to the port of Whitehaven from where it was shipped to eager customers all over the world.

It was the prosperity brought by the iron industry that gave birth to the town of Cleator Moor and contributed to one of its more unlikely characteristics.

Although the area already had strong links with Ireland (itinerant labourers had long been arriving by sea to work on the harvest) that was nothing compared with what happened next.

With the potato famine driving them from their homes in Ireland, and the prospect of rewarding work in the West Cumbrian mines, thousands upon thousands of Irishmen came to Cleator Moor – so many that the town became known as 'Little Ireland', a name it is still proud to carry to this day.

From a settlement of 763 in 1841, Cleator Moor grew to house 10,420 by 1871. Nearly 40 per cent of them were Irish, most of them Catholics.

It was hardly surprising that such an influx of Catholics into a traditionally reactionary place like West Cumbria – particularly at a time of the general anti-Catholicism of Victorian England – caused problems, and it is no surprise either that Cleator Moor experienced some of the earliest sectarian troubles in Britain.

In 1871 the Irish Protestant (and virulently anti-Catholic) preacher William Murphy toured the country inciting mobs to attack Catholic targets, and when he came to make a speech in Whitehaven the Catholic miners of Cleator Moor marched there to confront him.

Though faced with the threat of serious violence, Murphy refused to back down and he made his speech to a background of heckling and threats from his opponents and he got out of trouble only by being bundled away by his supporters.

He was not so lucky the next evening when the Irish miners turned up in even greater numbers. About 300 of them stormed the Oddfellows Hall, where he was speaking, and threw him down the stairs even before the meeting began.

He was not badly hurt but when he died in March of the next year most people accepted it was because of the injuries he sustained that night.

That was by no means the end of the area's sectarian troubles.

In July 1884 local protestants, led by no fewer than eight bands, commemorated the Battle of the Boyne by marching through Cleator Moor, past the Catholic church to Wath Brow where they held their assembly.

The town's Irish miners, seeing this as a deliberately provocative move, were waiting for them, so that when the Orangemen made their way back to the train station they were attacked by groups of local men throwing stones.

The Protestants did not hesitate to use their superior weapons – some of them carrying revolvers, cutlasses and pikes – and a local postal messenger, Henry Tumelty, a 17-year-old Catholic, was shot in the head and killed.

Many others were injured and the ill feeling continued for years, though these days there is, happily, no obvious sign of it.

Just about the only display of any past allegiance to Ireland comes in the name and colours of the local football team – Cleator Moor Celtic, founded by Irish immigrants in 1909, still play in the green and white hoops of their more illustrious and politically inspired cousins Glasgow Celtic, though for them it has never mattered whether a player was Catholic or Protestant.

Nor has there ever been any sectarian significance to the town's other major sports club – Wath Brow Hornets, whose superb little stadium and sports centre I passed half way up the hill from where I parked the Bongo.

The Hornets are one of the things this place has to be proud of.

They are an amateur rugby league club which for years has punched well above its weight on the national stage, and even those of us who have little or no interest in the sport know that they have often taken on and beaten the much bigger and more glamorous professional clubs of the big towns and cities further south.

These days Cleator Moor doesn't have much else to shout about, for sadly not even the area's vast reserves of iron ore could last forever, and with the mineral's extraction becoming more and more difficult, mines began to close.

Although the First World War and its desperate need for the iron to make weapons brought some respite, Cleator Moor's golden age was beginning to fade by the early 1900s.

And the rather sad, down at heel place we know today was on its way.

Still, the town does have many fine mementoes of those times, and I made sure that my walk took me past all of them.

At the top of the hill I turned away from the town centre and turned left towards the much older village of Cleator.

A row of dozens of terraced houses line one side of this street, each with an uninterrupted view across the valley to the Lake District.

A few, were nicely kept, obviously much loved by their owners, with pretty curtains at their windows and glistening, freshly doorsteps and glossy paintwork, but most just wore a uniform drabness of grey or dirty beige and looked rather sad.

In another place – like the harbourside cottages of Tobermory, for example, or the cottages lining the hill above Bristol's historic docks – they would have been carefully painted in a paintbox of pastel shades and photographed by a thousand tourists but here . . .

All they needed was some love and attention.

And, it has to be said, money.

Across the road a small memorial reminds us of a different sort of suffering.

A plaque commemorates six airmen who died on the fells near Cleator Moor after crashing their planes during training during World War II, reminding us that hatred was capable of wreaking its havoc even here, hundreds of miles from the front line.

The imposing Roman Catholic church of St Mary's carries much the same message for anyone aware of the area's sectarian past.

This solid-looking church – much bigger and far grander than might be expected in a poor West Cumbrian town – was one of more than 100 Catholic churches designed by Edward Welby Pugin (son of the man who designed the Houses of Parliament) and consecrated in 1872 ironically, the same year that anti-Catholic rabble-rouser William Murphy died after being thrown down the stairs in Whitehaven.

The church nestles into one corner of a huge and very ornate graveyard, which leads one way to a meditative Stations of the Cross walk and the other to a bizarre little man-made cave which at first sight seems totally at odds to its surroundings.

This is Our Lady's Grotto, a replica of the very much more famous grotto at Lourdes in France, whose construction an imaginative priest organised to give his parish's many unemployed men something useful to do during the depression of the 1920s.

It was built with rocks mostly dug up from the local mines but includes one that was brought from the real Lourdes grotto.

The priest's idea was that, in the early 1900s, when international travel was not as easy as it is now, the Cleator grotto would become a place of pilgrimage for people in this country who were unable to go to France, and indeed it worked, at least for a short time.

Catholics from Cumbria and the North-West of England no doubt found it an attractive proposition, but whether those further south looked upon a remote corner of West Cumbria any easier to get to than South West France is of course debatable.

Just half a mile down the road from the Catholic Church is the Anglican one – St Leonard's, which not surprisingly has a somewhat longer history than St Mary's.

This one dates back to around 1100, in the reign of King Henry I, and though it has undergone numerous changes in its 900 year history it has all the sense of history and spirituality that you would expect of such a place,

I could tell you that its 12th century chancel was built of sandstone blocks on a chamfered plinth or that above the 20th century windows (replicas of the original ones that dated back back to the 16th century) is a roof slated with coped gables and apex crosses . . . but what really interested me was its organ.

This fine instrument was built specially for St Leonard's by Harrison & Harrison, a firm founded in the late 1800s by my wife's great grandfather.

Harrisons, now based in Durham, are reckoned to be the finest organ makers in the world. Their work can be found in some of the world's greatest cathedrals and concert halls – everywhere from York Minster and Canterbury Cathedral to Stockholm City Hall and Seoul Cathedral, and from the Royal Festival Hall to the chapels of Durham prison and Eton College – and in hundreds of smaller churches and even private houses.

Even though I can't stand organ music (I once made my polite excuses and left a Harrison and Harrison anniversary celebration because it would have meant listening to an hour of it) it is always a thrill to find one of their organs in some of the least likely places.

And Cleator Moor is surely less likely than most . . .

A track behind the church took me past the sewage works, past the cricket ground (the village team once won the national championship at Lords) and into a world which contained many more reminders of Cleator Moor's past.

In its mining heyday Cleator Moor had two stations – one on the Whitehaven, Cleator and Egremont Railway, and another on the Cleator and Workington Junction Railway – and in between them ran several smaller branch lines linking individual mines with the rail network.

In 1923 both stations were closed to passengers and though the goods lines struggled on into the 1950s, they too eventually closed, leaving the decaying remains of old railway lines which have now been converted into the labyrinth of footpaths and cycle tracks that now crisscross the area.

Enough of the old railway detritus – a mysterious piece of iron here, a bit of concrete there – is left, along with some imaginative modern sculptures, to give some idea of just how busy this area would have been, and, in a nice touch, the modern cast iron signposts have been made in a style that would not have been out of place 100 years ago.

Eventually the path I had chosen deposited me right back in the heart of the town. And yes, there is no escaping the fact that it has seen better times.

And yet it is still trying.

In the town square – which with its impressive buildings and fabulous iron work would be packed with happy tourists drinking at pavement cafes in a more popular (and warmer) place a few hundred miles further south – are three sculptures by Conrad Atkinson, an artist of international repute who was born in Cleator Moor in 1940.

They are a memorial to the mining community, commissioned by Cleator Moor Town Council and dedicated by Neil Kinnock, in 1988 while he was leader of the Labour Party.

Nearby is an impressive memorial fountain to John Stirling, a mine owner from the early 1900s who was hugely admired for the amount of money he put back into the community and the good work he did in making life better for its inhabitants by building them schools, hospitals and churches.

And outside the library is a blue plaque reminding us that the artist L. S. Lowry often stayed in Cleator Moor and painted pictures of several of its buildings, including the bank and even the fish and chip shop.

There is, though, nothing to celebrate one more thing about Cleator Moor that is surely worthy of note and these days might be most important of all.

On my walk around the town, down its busy streets and never-quite-deserted footpaths, every person I met smiled and said hello.

That's not something that can be said about very many towns in the Lake District.

24
X-treme Triathlon

I always knew I was going to have a problem when my A-Z of the Lake District reached X.

For there is, unsurprisingly, nowhere in Cumbria – no pretty village, no towering mountain and no tumbling stream – whose name begins with the 24th letter of the alphabet.

China has Xi'an, Mexico has Xalapa, the USA has Xenia and even good old Belgium has a small village called Xhoffraix but a search across the whole of the UK reveals absolutely nothing.

Friends, aware of my predicament, did their best to help.

One suggested I might like to spend the night with the Bongo parked under the sign for a hospital's X-ray department (which might have been a good plan had there been any hospitals within the Lake District boasting such a facility), several had the idea of simply finding somewhere to park at any crossroads of my choosing and a couple proposed throwing a dart at a map of Cumbria and camping wherever it landed in an X-marks-the-spot sort of way.

In the end though I found the answer myself, thanks to a casual conversation with one of my sportier friends.

An event called the X-Treme Triathlon – described as the world's toughest such event – was being held in the Lake District.

So parking beside the course and waving in friendly fashion to the athletes as they passed was probably as close as I was going to get to spending the night in somewhere beginning with X.

I discovered that the X involved a swim across the top end of Windermere, followed by a 112-mile bike ride around the Lake District, taking in all its toughest mountain passes, and then, as if that wasn't enough, it would end with a marathon distance run up and down Scafell Pike, England's highest mountain.

I knew that this was my only chance to do X, out of sequence though it was. The X-Treme Triathlon happened on only one day each year, and I had to be there even though I was only up to F at that time (I had just been to Far Sawrey and had yet to visit Gowbarrow).

I studied the course of the race, and immediately discounted some sections on the grounds that, with some roads being closed for it, I might be chased away from my chosen parking spot by some high-vis jacket-wearing jobsworth . . . or, worse, find myself trapped for hours on the far side of a barricade.

So I fell back on one of my favourite roads – the steep 2½ mile hill that leads from Ambleside to the top of the Kirkstone Pass, known as The Struggle.

There were several places to park alongside it, without the risk of causing an obstruction to any passing cyclists – including the excellent lay-by, overlooking Windermere lake, which I had used on my first A-Z Bongo Night many months before.

But the most interesting one, I reckoned, would be the one shaped like a small quarry, half way up one of the steepest sections (at its worst The Struggle hits a gradient of 1 in 5), which would be the best vantage point for anyone wanting to witness the sheer savagery of the event.

I arrived there on the evening before the race was due to pass, early enough to bag the place for myself and deter anyone with similar ideas.

I parked the Bongo on a surprisingly level piece of ground, but with its bonnet pointing towards Ambleside, so that even without getting out I would have a fine view of any cyclists slogging up the hill from the valley below.

I passed a couple of hours just sitting in one of my folding armchairs, doing the things I always do on Bongo Nights – reading a book, playing my guitar and painting a watercolour of the stupendous view in front of me.

And I could very happily have spent the whole evening there until it became dark and it was time to go to bed.

But the knowledge that, just a quarter of a mile away, at the top of the hill, was the Kirkstone Pass Inn, an ancient and welcoming pub that boasts of being the highest in Cumbria, was too big a temptation.

So I started up the hill on foot towards it.

It was a stiff climb – made stiffer by the intense heat of the hottest evening of the year – and, though I like to think I am reasonably fit, I had to pause several times, gasping for breath.

And this, I told myself, was where an army of cyclists would be coming next morning as they set out on their punishing tour of the Lake District.

'Madness!' I told the smiling barman as I reached the pub, red-faced and sweating. 'It takes a particular type of lunacy to choose to ride a bike up there. It was bad enough just walking it!'

The barman misunderstood me, and thought I had walked all the way from Ambleside.

'No, I've got a campervan parked just down there in the little quarry,' I told him, quietly glowing with the knowledge that he thought I might be capable of walking so far up such a steep hill.

'You would be more than welcome to stay overnight in our car park,' he told me. 'It might be more comfortable than where you're parked at the moment.'

Suddenly my little quarry hideaway did not seem so perfect after all.

The luxury of parking in the pub car park – from which the views were not just even better than those from lower down, but also more commanding of the road up which the cyclists would be coming next morning – was too much of a temptation.

'I'll just finish this,' I said, nodding towards the pint that stood on the bar, 'then I'll go and fetch the van. Then I'll be back for another pint and some food. Perfect!'

I walked back down the hill – a very much easier undertaking than walking up it – and found that, on the steepest section, someone had written supposedly encouraging messages in white paint on the tarmac for the benefit of the cyclists who would be straining their way up next morning.

'Go Gav Go,' said one, and a rather less uplifting 'Wake up Steve' said another.

In that baking heat – and knowing it was likely to be hotter still tomorrow – both Gav and Steve had my unstinting admiration.

I did not know what time they and their fellow triathletes would be arriving the next day – just that they would start their day with a 2.4 mile swim around a bay at the northern end of Windermere at the unearthly hour of 4.30 in the morning.

I had no idea how long that might take them, but guessed that if they could swim at a fast walking pace they could be out of the water and on their bikes within little more than half an hour.

Another half hour – another guess! – for them to come through Ambleside and on up the long slog of The Struggle and, I reckoned, the fittest of them could be arriving at my the top quite well before 6am.

So when I moved the Bongo up the hill to the pub car park I manoeuvred it alongside a wall, so that from the driver's seat I had an uninterrupted view of the steepest parts of The Struggle as it wound its way up from Ambleside.

That meant that in the morning I would be able to keep a watch on the road from the comfort of the van, and only get out when I could see the cyclists approaching.

For now, though, I was happy to sit outside.

The evening sunshine was still warm enough for plenty of people in their T-shirts and shorts to be sitting outside at the picnic tables looking down at the valley, so I went into the pub to fetch another pint and to tell the barman that I had taken up his offer of a place in his car park.

A short time later I was tucking into a generous plateful of lamb (I always reckon that's a good bet at any pub in Cumbria, because if they don't know how to cook lamb there where do they?) while watching the day's clear blue sky turn a faint pink as the evening closed in around the mountains.

When the evening turned too cool to stay outside, I moved into the Bongo and listened to the radio – knowing that if I spent the whole evening in the pub I would end up drinking far more than was good for a man who looked like having to be up and about by what by my definition were the small hours.

Late on, though, I went back into the pub (although I am happy whenever necessary to hop over a wall or hedge for nature's necessities, a well maintained toilet complete with towel, hot water and soap was a luxury well worth pursuing) and ordered a whisky.

'We've got this one,' he said, gesturing towards a Speyside single malt that I had not tried before.

'Or,' in a less enthusiastic voice, 'we've got this one. It's a new one. Made here in the Lake District.'

I looked at him with some surprise, having never heard of a home-grown Cumbrian whisky.

'Not that I'd recommend it,' he continued, rolling his eyes towards the ceiling.

'Say no more, thanks, I'll stick with the Scotch,' I told him.

With only a couple of other people left in the bar, the barman had time for a chat.

He told me he had not known about the X Triathlon until I had told him about it, but he was not surprised because the Kirkstone Pass was on the route of virtually every cycling event in the Lake District, and there were plenty of them.

'We do get a lot,' he said with an air of exasperation. 'And they all seem to pass here very early in the morning. And they all seem incapable of doing it without making an awful lot of noise.'

I could tell that there had been problems in the past, and that with a gentle nudge he would be prepared to tell me about them.

'Noise – from bikes? The riders gasping for breath as they come up the hill, I suppose!'

'Not it's not the cyclists themselves,' he said. 'They're too busy to make a noise. It's their friends. They come here to the top of the hill and make a hell of a racket, shouting and cheering and whistling. And don't even mention the bloody cowbells!

'They've seen it on the telly with the Tour de France and reckon they have to do the same thing here.

'They could do it half a mile down the hill – or half a mile further on – but they do it right outside our pub, where people are trying to sleep. And they just don't seem to care.'

I returned to the Bongo and slept well . . . until the first car full of supporters swept into the car park soon after 5.30am.

And the barman was right – they just didn't care how much noise they made!

Four of them jumped out, one clutching a banner made from an old bed sheet, proclaiming 'Go go go!' in blood-red letters, and ran across the gravel to the top of the hill like a gang of over-excited teenagers on their way to a football match.

Half a dozen more cars followed, their occupants making no concession to anyone who might be sleeping in the pub . . . or in any of the four campervans they had parked alongside.

There were, it's true, no cowbells – but one man made up for their lack by running up and down the hill crazily beating a saucepan with a metal spoon.

I got dressed and alighted from the Bongo just (as I could tell from the cacophony of the spectators) as the first cyclist began his ascent of the final, steepest part of the hill.

As he pedalled determinedly towards the summit, his supporters ran alongside him whooping and hollering and, in one man's case anyway, beating out an appropriate rhythm on the saucepan.

For me it was interesting – the first time I had witnessed such a spectacle – and therefore not annoying.

I had, after all, deliberately chosen this Bongo Night so I could experience whatever was involved in an extreme cycle race, so – apart from having to get up at a time when I would normally have been fast asleep – I had no cause for complaint.

I was aware though that not everybody would have been sharing that view.

And by the time a few more cyclists had made it up the hill – each one accompanied by just as much whooping, hollering and cymbal-like crashing – the hotel staff, on behalf of their customers had had enough.

A youngish man – who, for no particular reason, I took to be a chef – came out of the staff quarters and walked the few yards to the crowd of spectators.

His anger, as I could tell, was bubbling quietly below the surface, but he was, I could also tell, supremely polite.

All I heard of his conversation was 'We have people here who have paid good money and are trying to sleep,' and for a few moments there was something approaching silence.

But then two more cyclists came into view around the corner near where I had parked the night before, and the whole thing started again.

It went on for about an hour, with the last few athletes arriving on foot, pushing their bikes and looking totally dispirited, as they reached the welcome sanctuary of the almost-flat road in front of the pub.

Then, as quickly as they had arrived – but making much less noise – the supporters sped away, clutching their saucepan and blood-red banner, to (presumably) go through the whole thing again to annoy someone further on along the course.

I turned on the gas, lit the burners and cooked myself bacon, egg, mushroom, fried bread and tomatoes.

And as I sat eating it in the early morning sun there was not a sound to be heard.

25
Yewdale

I see the Lake District as a posh house with many rooms – each one decorated in a slightly different style to the others.

There is the room containing the area around the Northern lakes – Ullswater and Mungrisdale, say – which is like a quiet and comfortable sitting room, full of beautifully upholstered armchairs and plumped up cushions, the sort of room to which you'd like to escape at the end of a hard day.

There's the area around Keswick and Derwentwater – a busy kitchen of a place, with people constantly coming and going and making themselves mugs of tea without ever taking their muddy boots off.

There's Windermere and Bowness, the games room of the house – noisy and bustling, where the kids bring their boisterous friends and you're forever popping in to tell them to tone things down a bit.

There's Coniston and Hawkshead, which have the air of an old man's study, a bit dark and faded, but that's something you forgive because you know important things have been done in the past even though you can't see much sign of it these days.

And in between there is a maze of passages and corridors though which people hurry, without paying much attention to the paintings on the walls, as they make their way from one room to another.

My point being that, while the Lake District is one wonderful, beautiful place, it is in fact made up of several smaller ones, each with its own identity and each very different from the others.

This was something that became more and more clear to me the further I got through my A-Z of the Lake District, visiting parts of the area to which I had not been for years, if at all.

And my choice for Y took me to one of those long neglected corridors, a place I had not noticed before in my journeying around the more popular 'rooms'.

Yewdale is a pretty valley, whose best bit is not much more than three miles long, linking Tarn Hows and Coniston, and overlooked by most of the hordes of tourists who flock to those two honeypots.

I discovered that the National Trust, which owns much of the land in these parts, recommended a circular walk – a mere 4.3 miles – that 'takes in the charming Yewdale valley' and 'gains enough height to provide good views of the landscape, but stays low enough to be not too demanding'.

As an introduction to a place I did not know, it seemed as good as any . . .

And what an ideal spot for a Bongo Night it turned out to be.

I am not going to recommend any of the National Trust's three car parks at Tarn Hows because it has now made it clear that it does not approve of people like me parking their campervans overnight on its property.

And anyway, even though the biggest of those car parks has a few hidden corners in which a van might be parked safely out of sight, why risk the wrath of some passing Trust warden when there are numerous other even better places nearby?

The one I chose was on the narrow and winding one-way road leading from that car park down the hill to Coniston village.

Not a quarter of a mile from the top, so before too much height has been lost, is an almost flat Bongo-sized ledge at the side of the road, pointing west, with a wonderful view across the valley to the great mountains of Wetherlam and the Old Man of Coniston.

Try as you might you will probably not find a more dramatic spot in which to spend the night in the Lake District.

From there it was easy to walk a little way back up the road to pick up the National Trust's recommended route.

The path plunges down the steep hillside, almost following the cascading course of Tom Gill (which, for reasons probably known only to himself, the celebrated Victorian art critic and all-round intellectual John Ruskin decided should be renamed Glen Mary) all the way to a picturesque bridge.

Ruskin's intervention gives a small clue to what I see as one of this area's problems: It is largely an invention, dreamed up by Victorians who believed they could improve on nature.

Tarn Hows, glorious landscape though it is, is a fabrication.

And so is much of the land around it.

Not that it bothers the half million people who visit it every year, of course, but much as I loved it as I walked through it on my way down to Coniston, I could not rid my mind of the fact that it was not quite real.

Until the 1860s most of the Tarn Hows area was open land used by local farmers to graze their animals in much the same way as other areas of the Lake District are farmed to this day.

It was only when the Marshall family, who owned vast chunks of enclosed land – including several farms and quarries – in the neighbourhood, used the controversial Enclosure Act of 1862 to take possession of what until then had been common land that things began to change.

James Garth Marshall, the MP son of an industrialist who had made his fortune from textiles in the Yorkshire mills, decided the landscape was not quite to his liking so he embarked on a series of 'improvements', including the planting of thousands of trees, the moving of several big rocks that he deemed to be not quite in the right place and the building of a dam to increase the size of one of the three tarns there.

It quickly became a favourite beauty spot, beloved by picnickers in the summer and ice skaters in winter, and it soon found itself on the must-see list for people taking charabanc trips from the burgeoning tourist centres of Ambleside and Windermere.

In the late 1920s the Marshall family decided to sell the estate, all 4,000 acres of it, and Beatrix Potter, of Peter Rabbit fame, whose great grandfather had once owned one of the farms on it, initially bought the lot for £15,000, knowing she could only afford it if she managed to sell half of it on.

This she did when the National Trust raised enough money to buy most of the land she did not want to keep, and she completed the deal by giving away the last part anonymously and agreeing to carry on managing the land on its behalf.

My walk took me through the land that was once owned by Beatrix Potter, including the picture-postcard beautiful, near-400-year-old Yew Tree Farm, which is said to be one of the most photographed farms in the north of England and is now an upmarket self catering holiday retreat where you can get married, if you have a mind to.

The walk took me down a gentle path, a shared footpath and cycle way, which clings to the lowest edge of the Yewdale Fells, with Yewdale Beck tumbling quietly and mostly unseen in the valley on the other side of the road to my left.

It was incredibly, unseasonably hot and I was glad of the shade from the trees above me.

The number of people I met – both walkers and cyclists – showed me that this was a popular path for people with far more energy than I.

I just wish that they had not left such a mess behind.

On a stretch of path that measured no more than two miles I counted seven black dog poo bags (five of them hanging from trees), 17 discarded plastic bottles (mostly Lucozade Sport), nine plastic sandwich wrappers and one large white supermarket carrier bag with its contents of used food cartons, drinks cans and crisp packets spilling from its mouth.

I stopped at a spot with a lovely view of an ancient lime kiln, sitting on a fallen oak with an elaborate collection of fungi at its base, and as I unscrewed my flask for a gulp of tea noticed that I had perched beside a pile of toilet paper, clearly and stomach-churningly used.

I continued down the path towards Coniston, gloomy and disheartened.

I was debating with myself the merits of banning all tourists from the Lake District when I had to step aside for a cyclist.

I have no doubt that I glowered at him.

'Good morning, sir,' he said with the smile of a man without a care. 'And thank you.'

I stepped back onto the path just in time to have to step off it again for his girlfriend.

Her smile lit up my morning.

'Thank you very much,' she sang. 'Have a lovely day.'

'You too,' I called.

'I already am, thank you.'

And with that she was gone, pedalling hard to catch up her boyfriend, and leaving me feeling as guilty as hell for the very large brush with which I had tarred the whole tourist population.

I had not intended to go into Coniston. I could have taken another path leading back over the hills to Tarn Hows without ever having to go into the town.

But I was so hot I took a detour for an ice cream.

I found a path that I guessed led to the lakeside and the pier where, I knew, was a cafe.

What I did not guess was that the path would take me down to the river – Yewdale Beck – and then follow it until it emerged quietly and almost unnoticed under the trees into Coniston Water.

That seemed to give my walk extra justification. Following Yewdale Beck to its end could have been exactly what I had planned when I chose to do Y for Yewdale.

The beach at Coniston was like something from the Costa del Sol. People were everywhere – swimming, sunbathing, sitting on beach towels, playing with balls and frisbees, queueing for boats,

The bustle was as extraordinary as it was (for me at any rate) unexpected.

This was a side of the Lake District I almost always tried to avoid and nothing about it made me want to change my mind . . . except the strawberry ice cream milk shake which on a day as hot as this made everything else worthwhile.

I sat on a bench and quietly enjoyed not being part of the crowd.

Even so I got up and resumed my walk just as soon as the icy drink had done its job, heading back along the path upon which I had arrived, to find the one that would lead me back to Tarn Hows and the Bongo.

Somewhere along the way I went wrong, and found myself instead in the middle of the town, jostling with the tourists (yes, I know I was one too!) on the pavements outside the cafes and souvenir shops, stepping aside to avoid bicycles and taking care not to be hit by any of the cars whose drivers were more intent on finding somewhere free to park than missing people like me.

I spotted a graveyard with a path leading in the direction of where I knew I wanted to be, so went through the gate, hoping it would be a short cut, with a gate in the bushes at the other end.

Two gardeners, both armed with noisy strimmers, looked at me with neither interest nor amusement, just as they did a couple of minutes later when I walked back down the path, pretending I was looking for something since I did not want to admit that I was only there because I had been hoping to find a way out.

I wandered back, through the gravestones this time, rather than along the path, and came to one a little more ornate than the rest, with a garish blue bird painted in the corner.

DONALD MALCOLM CAMPBELL CBE
Queens Commendation for Brave Conduct
March 1921 - January 1967
Laid to rest September 2001
Whose achievements in world speed records
depict his courage in life and death

I had chanced upon the grave of the man who died on Coniston Water while trying to beat the world speed record.

He had reached 297mph in his boat Bluebird on the outward run – 21mph faster than the record he himself had set in Australia four years earlier – and was doing nearly 320mph on the return when he lost control and it flew head over heels and crashed horrifically upside down.

Bluebird was eventually raised from the lake bed in March 2001 and Campbell's body was recovered a little while later, and buried here in what I discovered was Coniston's new parish cemetery (the old one is alongside the church on the other side of the road).

Many people, I know, go to Coniston especially to pay their respects at this brave man's grave.

I felt a little ashamed that I had found myself there by accident, just because I had been looking for a short cut on a walk in the sunshine.

The path back to Tarn Hows, when I found it, led almost immediately uphill, and continued that way for half a mile.

It was not what I would have chosen in such heat, and it was only the sight of a small wood at the top of the hill – and the shade I knew it would give me – that kept me going.

It was a perfect place for a picnic and I sat under the trees enjoying both the view back over Coniston and the knowledge that I had got the worst over with.

The rest of the way back to where I had parked the Bongo was a delight, a gently undulating track that probably dated back many centuries, across fields, through trees, beside bubbling streams – this was all that I love most about the Lake District.

It was still extraordinarily hot and with a mile or so to go I lay down, hoping to go to sleep in the deep shade of a huge oak tree, just off the track.

I was disturbed by the sound of voices – half a dozen walkers, middle-aged and fully equipped for a day and, in emergency, a night on the fells.

'Hello,' I called, from my hideaway in the darkness.

'Waaaaaaghhh!' said one of the men, and as they continued down the path away from me I heard him talking to his friends.

'Bloody hell, scared me to death,' he said. 'Who was that? It was like a voice coming from hell.'

By the time I got back to the Bongo I had walked more than eight miles, almost double the 4.3 miles I had expected to do on the National Trust walk, and I was hot, thirsty and very tired.

I opened all the windows, pulled out the bed and lay down for a rest.

But not for the first time I discovered that while an afternoon nap in the Bongo is a very attractive idea, putting it into practice was much more difficult.

After ten minutes of lying there, realising sleep was not going to come, I got up . . . and went for a walk.

Being so close to Tarn Hows, one of the Lake District's most popular places, I could hardly miss the chance of finding what all the fuss was about.

What harm could another short walk do, after all?

I was helped along my way by an excellent rhubarb and ginger ice cream from a National Trust van in the car park (yes, here at Tarn Hows the Trust has its own ice cream van – 'every scoop helps the places you love') but it did not take long to realise that I was not really fit to walk the two miles around the tarns.

I was hot, I was tired, my feet were sore and despite the ice cream and all the water I had drunk throughout the day I was probably dehydrated.

I walked around Tarn Hows like a very old man, very slowly, and stopping to rest on every bench that had not been vandalised (and on a couple that had), and for once I was grateful for the crowds of tourists with their pushchairs, tricycles and zimmer frames who would have prevented me walking any faster even if I had been able to.

Back, eventually, at the Bongo, I opened all the windows, pulled out the bed . . . and slept soundly for half an hour.

The Z bends of Hardknott

Many years ago my mother, newly widowed after the too-early death of my Dad, surprised us all by going to the Lake District and staying alone in a hotel near Keswick.

It might not sound much, but for a grieving woman who for more than 30 years had hardly done anything without the man she loved at her side – and for whom staying in a hotel, even with him, had always been a pretty scary experience – it was an extraordinary achievement.

But then, as we were to discover, my Mum was made of tougher, more determined (some might say bloody-minded) stuff than any of us had imagined.

So we should not have been surprised that, when a know-all fellow guest at the hotel told her that the last thing she should do during her week in the Lakes was attempt to drive on its most challenging high passes, she took it as a challenge and headed immediately for Hardknott.

What that hotel guest had not known was that it was driving that was keeping my Mum going during those first years on her own. She had learned to drive as a teenager and had loved driving ever since – a passion she now displayed by driving for hundreds of miles (sometimes at rather greater speeds than we might have wished) because it was the only way she knew to escape her unhappiness. So it was inevitable that, when told that the Hardknott Pass might be beyond her, she took it as an invitation to prove that it wasn't.

The Hardknott Pass is, it must be said, a pretty difficult road – with one-in-three (that's 33% in modern parlance) hills, sharp Z-bends that almost double back on themselves and places where it is impossible to see approaching traffic because the road rises so steeply in front of you the bonnet on your own car obscures your view of any other.

And the fact that you reach it via the Wrynose Pass, which is almost as exhilarating and only slightly less hazardous, only adds to its attraction for those of us who, like my mother, enjoy driving to the extreme.

Hardknott is regularly voted one of the top ten most dangerous roads in Britain.

As one contributor to the Drive Tribe website says: 'I have driven all over Western Europe, including all the 9,000ft passes in the Alps and have never seen anything to rival the Hardknott Pass.'

And another says: 'It's so high up, the summit is actually 80 metres higher up than the top of the Shard in London. Imagine standing at the top of the Shard, how terrifying would that be? Now add 80 metres to it, along with poor weather conditions, narrow roads and nothing in the way of safety, and you can only imagine the emotions that would course through your mind and body as you reach the top of the Hardknott Pass.'

The Dangerous Roads website describes it as 'heart-stopping' and 'unnerving' and says it is 'the most brutal of the gruelling Lake District passes'. And warming to its theme it adds with, surely, just a touch of exaggeration: 'There are some narrow sections where if two vehicles have to pass each other one might have to reverse for some kilometres of winding narrow road to get to a place wide enough to pass.'

And that's just for ordinary cars. The idea of taking a campervan – or, worse, a motorhome – is frequently dismissed as ludicrous.

A member of one motorhome group writes on one of the many message board threads devoted to the subject: 'If you are thinking of attempting this in a camper van . . . don't. We saw a camper van in a bit of trouble as it seems they couldn't get the van round one of the hairpin bends.'

Some people even question the wisdom of building such a road in the first place – presumably not realising that it has been there for nearly 2,000 years.

The first road over the pass was built by the Romans in about AD 110 to link the fort at Ravenglass on the coast with their garrisons at Ambleside and Kendal so it was originally used entirely for military traffic.

When the Romans left Britain in the early 5th century it remained as an unpaved packhorse route, albeit a fast deteriorating one because of lack of upkeep, and was used for the transportation of lead and agricultural goods.

By the early Middle Ages, the road – by now finding a course slightly away from that favoured by the Romans – was known as the Waingate (cart road) and there is a record of a party of monks traversing it in an oxcart in the year 1138.

In the 1880s the English Lake District Association (an association of hoteliers) paid for improvements to the road in the hope that tourists would be attracted to come in the horse-drawn carriage equivalent of today's coach trips but within a few years the scheme was judged to be 'not the success that was anticipated' and the route fell into disrepair again.

Even so, the first motor vehicles managed to labour their way over the Hardknott and Wrynose passes shortly before the First World War and the route became something of a favourite among both cyclists and pioneering motorists.

All that ended in World War II when the War Office took over the the area and used it for tank training, thereby completely destroying the existing road surface – a blessing in disguise, as it turned out, because after the war the damage was repaired and the road given a proper tarmac topping so that for the first time there was a (relatively) easy way to get from one side to the other.

Even so, there are still several prominent road signs warning of the dangers at either end of the pass – 'Extreme caution,', 'Narrow route, severe bends' – and it would indeed be folly for anyone in a campervan to ignore them.

Anyone in a campervan that's not a Bongo, that is.

For as I have said before, one of the many joys of the Bongo is that it is small and nimble enough to go anywhere that an ordinary family car can go.

So, ignoring all the warnings and with supreme confidence that the Bongo would not be daunted by such a challenge, I set off on a trip that would take in the Kirkstone Pass (1,489ft) the Wrynose Pass (1,281ft) and the considerably more challenging Hardknott Pass (1,289ft).

The Wrynose Pass is a good place for a Bongo Night; the Hardknott Pass, because of the drama of its steep climbs and punishing Z-bends, is a great one.

I was heading for a place where a few years ago I spent one of my most memorable Bongo Nights – a place where before going to bed I had spent a couple of hours sitting on a huge rock in the evening sunshine, playing my guitar to an appreciative audience of sheep and gazing out at the distant Irish Sea.

It was in a small parking space beside the Hardknott Roman fort, an extraordinarily impressive site owned and cared for by English Heritage, a short walk from the road on the far side of the pass, where the steepest of the hills are replaced by something approaching not much more than a slope.

It was there that a passing driver stopped his car, wound down his window and told me: 'That must be the most beautiful place any man has ever played a guitar.'

I told him that indeed it was.

And as he drove away I heard him mutter: 'Lucky devil.'

But before I could get to the fort I had the Z-bends to contend with.

It's easy to think the worst must be over when, after successfully negotiating the challenge of Wrynose the twisting and turning road across the mountain turns into an unthreatening stretch across the lowlands of the valley.

But suddenly, almost before you've had a chance to catch your breath, the road rises again and you're faced with something steeper, sharper, more dramatic and more dangerous than anything that's come before.

A sharp zig to the right, then an even sharper zag to the left, then another zig quickly followed by another zag and a zig. . . these are indeed the Z-bends of Hardknott in all their glory.

I put the Bongo into bottom gear, pressed the 'hold' button to make sure it did not have any silly ideas of changing into second and put just a bit more pressure on the accelerator pedal.

If I were of a more fanciful state of mind I would say that the Bongo relished the chance to show what it could do.

Some might say the engine growled with the effort. I prefer to think that it was singing. In a deep baritone voice, the Bongo was singing with happiness, pleased at last to be given the chance to enjoy putting one on all those other vans – bigger, plusher, newer and a great deal more expensive – which did not have the ability or the courage to face such excitement.

There is no great skill demanded of a driver.

Just a willingness to take it steadily, to keep a careful watch on the road ahead and stop in good time for any traffic coming the other way, and to look out for any sharp rocks that might tear your tyres to shreds if you have to take the appropriate evasive action.

I can imagine that for someone who does his driving in the concrete confines of a big city, the whole experience might be terrifying (just as it might be for me if I were made to tackle Piccadilly Circus at rush hour on a Friday night).

But I'm lucky. I have spent all my life living in the country, where the roads are narrow, the hedges are high, the hills are steep and the bends are sharp, so driving up Hardknott is just an exaggerated way of doing what I've been doing for 50 years.

When we reached the top, I was smiling.

And I like to think the Bongo was smiling too.

It was something of a disappointment when we descended the other side, down to the rough layby that serves as the Roman fort's car park.

For that – magnificent though it was, with stupendous views across the valley to Scafell Pike – marked the end.

Not just the end of the Lake District, being as I was just a few miles from the western boundary of the National Park.

But, more than that, just a few miles from the end of my A-Z challenge. From Ambleside and Buttermere to Yewdale and the Z bends of Hardknott I had seen the very best that the Lake District had to offer – from the windswept wildness to the tacky souvenir shops, from the towering mountains to the exquisite hidden valleys, from the honeypots to the remote places that I like to think nobody knew about but me.

It was all done.

All over.

My A-Z adventure had been all I had hoped it would be. It had given me 26 memorable one-night holidays and 26 mini adventures. It had taken me to places I had never found before and introduced me to people I would never otherwise have met.

Lucky devil, indeed!

THE END

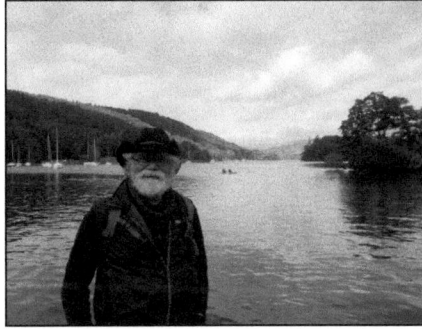

ABOUT THE AUTHOR

Richard Harris is a retired journalist and
one-time evening newspaper editor
who spent more than 40 years
in the UK provincial newspaper industry.
He grew up in Somerset and began his career
in Weston-super-Mare. He went on to work on
newspapers in Bristol and Nottingham before
moving to Carlisle 30 years ago.
He now lives in a small village in North Cumbria.

www.richardharrisnews.co.uk

BACK COVER: Eycott Hill (picture by Eddie Stephenson)